How to Make Your REALTOR® Get You the Best Deal

Durango, Colorado Edition

The following is a sample of the testimonials received on our various state editions:

This book is a wonderful road map for the ever-confusing world of real estate. It's like having your own personal coach in a box.

—Melissa Giovagnoli, Author, best-selling book, *Networlding*

. . . eminently readable. . . .

—Edwin J. Ricketts, Deputy Commissioner of the Arizona Department of Real Estate, 1991–1997

This book should be required reading for all Realtors® and for anyone serious about buying real estate.

—Peter J. McLaughlin, author of *Catch Fire: A Seven-Step Program to Ignite Energy, Defuse Stress and Power Boost Your Performance*

Life would have been much easier if I had this book to give to my buyers when I was out in the field. There are so many great ideas and so much information . . . all agents should carry copies in their briefcases.

—Dale Rector, Founder, Realty Executives

In life, it seems you don't get what you deserve, you get what you negotiate, and How to Make Your Realtor® Get You the Best Deal *gives you the necessary tools it takes to be able to be in the best possible position to negotiate in real estate. My hat is off to Jenny, Ken and their national consortium.*

—Mike Barnett, VP Technology of InternetCrusade (an organization that provides Realtor® training nationwide and provides tools to enhance communication between Realtors® and the public)

I read the entire Montana Edition over the weekend. It was fantastic. It was so insightful and full of such valuable information. So much of what you said has already helped me. Now I would like to take the most important step I read about: how to pick our Realtor®. Since we are out of the area, is there someone with your views and credentials that you can recommend?

—Tracie Kwiatkowski

In the Oklahoma Edition, two profoundly successful real estate agents have provided a simple guide through the often dark and confusing waters of home buying or selling. They demonstrate the impact of recent changes in the law and how those changes can affect the quality of representation one receives. Read this book and you will learn how to screen, select and then use your Realtor® in a way that Gets You the Best Deal.

—Steve Largent, U.S. Congressional
Representative, Oklahoma

Many Realtors® might put this down as too elementary, but I wish all my clients would review the simple steps provided here, and they could learn to be an effective part of the teamwork it takes to fulfill their dreams. This book has the exact things most buyers and sellers need to know, but are sometimes afraid to ask.

—John Foltz, President,
Realty Executives

I found your book to be very informative and easy to read. I will definitely recommend it to customers, especially those buying a home. It was a real eye-opener and fills a gap in our real estate section. Other books may have chapters on this topic, but your book is so concise and specific. I genuinely learned from your book (among other things, now I know what all those letters after your name stand for). Congratulations. Yours truly,

—Diane Eklund, Purchaser,
Powell's Books, Portland OR

This is a ground-breaking work for homebuyers. It is not only a quick read, but it puts the language of real estate in layman's terms. This book will do more to empower the homebuyer than anything else in print. I strongly recommend you buy this book before you even start looking at ads.

—Michael E. Houtari,
Corporate Attorney

How to Make Your REALTOR® Get You the Best Deal

Durango, Colorado Edition

A guide through the real estate purchasing process, from choosing a REALTOR® to negotiating the best deal for you!

by

Rick Lorenz

& Ken Deshaies

Gabriel Publications

Published by:
Gabriel Publications
14340 Addison St. #101
Sherman Oaks, California 91423
(818) 906-2147 Voice
(818) 990-8631 Fax
www.GabrielBooks.com

ISBN #1-891689-39-8
Library of Congress Catalog Card Number: 2003107288

Distributed by: Partners Book Distributors
Publisher: Rennie Gabriel
Editors: Davida Sims and Renee Ergazos
Typography: SDS Design, info@sds-design.com
Cover Design: Dale Schroeder, SDS Design

Manufactured in the United States of America.

Contents

Part One: The Home-Buying Process: A Brief History

Part Two: A New Law for the People

Part Three: Let's Get Started

Part Four: Getting Your Home

Part Five: Other Considerations

Appendices

Acknowledgment

We must start by acknowledging our good friend, a fellow REALTOR® and e-PRO, Mollie Wasserman. Mollie is a true pioneer in the area of real estate and the Internet, and we are so lucky that she was willing to provide a special chapter for us on this topic. This is a very important subject in today's real estate transactions and we urge all of our readers to make sure they are prepared to deal with both the benefits and limitations of the Internet.

Acknowledgments by Rick Lorenz

Life is a journey not a destination. When I reflect on my real estate career, many people have been there to give me guidance, counsel and encouragement. Occasionally I needed a kick in the pants, and thankfully that kick was properly administered. I would like to give credit to those who have walked the path with me.

Posthumously, to **Dean Suttle and Joe Shober** who took me under their wings back in the 70s. They taught me real estate from the ground up: residential, commercial, land, small ranches, and even mining property. Their motto was always "You do what is right. If the deal falls apart, it falls apart. Don't ever force a transaction." It was an honor to be trained by these Durango real estate legends.

My wife, **Debi**, has been by my side giving encouragement when I couldn't figure out how to put thoughts into words on paper. She has also been there at home when I was still at the office working. To paraphrase and slightly alter an old proverb "An understanding wife is more valuable than gold."

My business partner, CPA and most importantly friend, **Jim Hugins,** has witnessed my entire real estate career and has been a terrific confidante in shaping my practice.

Lastly, to **Allen Hainge**, the founder of the CyberStars™. He has brought me full throttle into the computer and technology age in real estate, allowing me to provide high touch as well as high tech services.

Most importantly, I thank the hundreds of families who have trusted me in the single most important purchase of their life.

Acknowledgments by Ken Deshaies

There are those without whom this book would not have been written and they deserve more than the recognition given here. Their faith in me, at times, exceeded my own.

Sloan Bashinski, who in 1984, published a book called *Home Buyers: Lambs to the Slaughter?*,which has served as an inspiration to me in my real estate practice.

My friend and teacher, **J. Albert Bauer**, who was the attorney for the Summit Association of REALTORS®, a member of the Approved Forms Committee for the Colorado Real Estate Commission, and remains a great trainer of REALTORS®. "Jay" was kind enough to edit the book with an eye to the legal and technical issues. His contributions were invaluable.

My wife and business partner, **Mary**, who helped with the typing and editing. In addition to carving time out of her hectic schedule, she made me find the time I claimed I didn't have.

My sister-in-law, **Anna Warner**, who became the first reader of the book and edited it with insight and sensitivity.

My publisher, **Rennie Gabriel**, who constantly prodded without pushing, and who was a constant source of inspiration and ideas.

The **hundreds of clients** whom Mary and I have worked with through the years and who have provided the fodder for this book.

Patricia McDade, founder and inspirational leader of The Entrepreneurial Edge, who helped me understand that anything is possible.

And my business coach, **Bill Rogers**.

Disclaimer

We've tried, we really have. We have attempted to ensure that everything said here is accurate and relevant. But laws change, circumstances vary, and there is always the possibility for error. Using the guidance offered here, along with your selection of a competent real estate professional, you should feel confident in purchasing or selling real estate. If your situation is complicated by any of a myriad of factors, such as the property being a business, farm or ranch, or if it has septic tank, well, soil, or title problems, we recommend you consult with a REALTOR® who specializes in that area. Or, you may want to hire an attorney or other professional who can assist with the specifics involved.

About gender usage: In order to avoid numerous grammatical messes and to make the reading flow better, we have chosen to write this book as gender neutral as possible. We have used *they* and *their,* even if it was one person, instead of *he or she, his and hers* and so on.

About the term *Realtor®*: This is a registered trademark of the National Association of REALTORS® (NAR), and anyone who uses that term as part of their professional identity must be a member, not only of the NAR but also of their local and state associations. We always encourage both buyers and sellers to seek out the services of a Realtor® when possible. However, even though we recommend the use of a Realtor®, we know there are many small communities in the country where there are no Realtors®. Many times throughout this book we will refer to "agent," "licensee," "real estate salesperson," "broker," and so forth. We do this because anyone who holds a real estate sales license must abide by laws, which we will cover in Chapter 4. These laws apply to ALL real estate agents in the United States, not just Realtors®. To make the text easier to read we may also show the registration mark as Realtor®. Please see Chapter 7 for a more complete explanation of this designation.

Again, please consult with a professional in your state based on your situation. You can also reach the authors directly through the contact information provided at the beginning and end of the book. Also, feel free to contact the authors for a referral to a Realtor® in your area.

Foreword by the Publisher

When Sloan Bashinski wrote his groundbreaking book, *Home Buyers: Lambs to the Slaughter?* in 1984, the rules and laws were vastly different than they were when the first edition of this book was first written in 2000.

When Ken Deshaies and I originally consulted with Sloan about updating his book, we found the differences too daunting and a transition too confusing. We felt that as the reader, you care more about how to navigate in today's world and care less about what occurred in the past. Therefore, this book is dedicated to you, and it attempts to provide the tools to make buying or selling a home today a process that works for you.

In the hundreds of cases where the authors have represented buyers and sellers and observed hundreds of other transactions where other agents were involved, they have found one overriding factor, which can make the difference between a successful home transaction and one that is less than satisfactory: service.

The difference in the level of service provided by your agent and the attitude they project will translate into one of two situations at the closing table: Either the consumers are knowledgeable, informed and pleased, or because of last-minute surprises, they are frustrated, angry, combative, and resentful and they can even walk out of the transaction. No one wants to be surprised where money is concerned, especially when it's costing you more than you thought. Even a certain degree of incompetence can be overcome by a real estate professional who tries hard, is not afraid to ask lots of questions and places your best interests ahead of their commission.

This book is clearly biased, as all books are that advocate a position. It represents the authors' view of the world. Though it is a view we feel is valid, other views exist, and some are very contradictory. We feel buyers and sellers make better clients when they are fully educated about the transaction. We also feel it is time that buyers are represented in the real estate transaction. We believe this book will show you how to get the most service from a real estate professional and how to ensure that key person is on your side. We hope you find it valuable.

—Gabriel Publications
A division of The Financial Coach, Inc.
Book Publishing, Corporate Training,
and Business Coaching

info@GabrielBooks.com

About the Authors

Rick Lorenz is a broker for the Wells Group Real Estate Brokerage in Durango, Colorado. He began his real estate career in 1977 and has earned many designations that rank him among the top five percent of Realtors® worldwide. He is a Certified Residential Specialist (CRS), an Accredited Buyer Representative (ABR), a Graduate of the Realtors® Institute (GRI), a Certified Internet Real Estate Professional (e-PRO) and an Allen F. Hainge Real Estate CyberStar™ (an elite group of Realtors® who have proven they generate a significant portion of their business through the use of today's technology). His excellence and accomplishments in the real estate business come from his commitment to learning and keeping abreast of changes in the industry. As a result, Rick has spent over 600 hours in continuing education classes in real estate related courses.

Due to his hours of training and passion for his field, Rick has become one of Durango's most experienced brokers. He has attained special skills in marketing, negotiating and contract writing as well as many other areas of buying and selling real estate. He is also the owner, builder and developer of a seven-million dollar residential development near Detroit, Michigan. In addition, he has successfully closed over 1,000 real estate transactions from small lots to large multi-million dollar commercial tracts and ranches. Rick is also a specialist at 1031 tax deferred exchanges. With his extensive knowledge and resources, as well as his dedication to his clients, Rick provides service that his clients can count on.

Rick is not only a dedicated and resourceful professional, he is also committed to giving back to the community in any way he can. He has spent countless hours working on behalf of the local board of Realtors® as the chairman of assorted committees as well as serving on the local board of directors. In addition, Rick and his wife Debi are facilitators for a divorce/separation recovery group called Divorce-Care.

When not in his office, Rick can be found spending time with his wife and playing with his four grandchildren. Rick has also been blessed to share his voice in his church choir. He is a former director and instructor for the Durango/Purgatory Adaptive Ski Association and actually moved from Michigan to Colorado early in his life because he fell in love with the mountains.

To Reach Rick Lorenz
(800)955-0259 ext. 145
Rick@BuyDurango.com or
see page 149

Ken Deshaies is a REALTOR® in Colorado. Ken is an Accredited Buyer Representative (ABR), Certified Residential Specialist (CRS), Graduate from the REALTOR® Institute (GRI), one of the first 500 REALTORS® in the country to become a Certified Internet Real Estate Professional (e-PRO500), is a Real Estate Cyberspace Specialist (RECS) and is an Allen F. Hainge CyberStar™—an elite group of REALTORS® who have proven that they generate a significant portion of their business through the use of current technology. He was named CyberStar of the Year for 2002, and elected President of the Summit Association of REALTORS® for 2003. He served on the committee for the Colorado Association of REALTORS® that spearheaded the change in agency laws effective in 2003. For several years, Ken served as the chairperson of the Professional Standards Committee of the Summit Association of REALTORS®, the committee that oversees the ethical conduct of association members.

Ken is an owner/broker and works in partnership with his wife, Mary. He began his real estate career in Denver in 1992 and has worked in Summit County since 1994. Located an hour west of Denver, Summit County is home to four ski resorts and the highest fresh-water sailing lake in the United States. While purchasing resort real estate is similar in many ways to buying in a metropolitan area it offers unique problems for locals and first-time homebuyers as well as for out-of-area investors.

Prior to real estate, Ken owned a private investigations firm for 12 years in Denver, employing and supervising as many as seven investigators and serving for a period as the President of the Professional Private Investigators Association of Colorado. In this work, he conducted numerous investigations into real estate transactions and claims of fraud. Many of the stories in this book are from Ken's experiences, both before and after he became a REALTOR®. During much of this time, he was also a member of the Win/Win Business Forum of Denver and was its president for a year and a half.

To Reach Ken Deshaies
Ken@SnowHome.com
or
see page 149

Preface

by Rick Lorenz

When I meet with buyers, I have a small bucket containing 16 wooden sticks. Each four-sided stick is painted white and has words written on it. The words are questions that I have posed regarding the type of property my clients wish to buy. One stick asks "number of bedrooms/ bathrooms" while another asks "approximate square footage." Other sticks contain two sets of descriptive words about the kinds of property my clients wish to see—"city lot or acreage," and "views of snowcapped mountains" or "I'm from Iowa so any view will do." Then there are sticks with the options of "city utilities required" or "well and septic are fine." Although these are just examples, I hope you get the idea.

In order for me to find my clients their ideal property, both of us need to know the answers to all 16 questions. No perfect property exists, so even if a client wants to build from scratch, my goal is to find them the property with the most sticks.

You may have noticed that I did not mention price. Although price is one of the sticks, it varies in importance to every buyer. If you are a first time home buyer needing to cash in pop bottles in order to have enough money to cover closing costs, then the price stick is likely the most important. On the other hand, I have many clients who, when presented with a 14 stick home, are more than agreeable to exceed their previously stated budget.

When looking at homes, it is not at all uncommon for clients to say to me "that was a 12 or 14 stick house." When I hear that, I know that we have communicated effectively and I am doing my job correctly. On the other hand, I hope never to hear from my buyers, "that one was just eight sticks," because that would mean I didn't properly interview the buyer regarding their likes and dislikes. I certainly don't want to misuse a buyer's time looking at six or eight stick homes when we both know that such a property would never be suitable.

Introduction

What Could Possibly Go Wrong?

Life would be great if we didn't have to practice diligence in nearly every action we take. From setting up your bedside alarm clock, to purchasing stereos and appliances, to buying a home, we have a primary responsibility to be aware of the potential pitfalls. Unfortunately, most people pay less attention to the process of buying their home than they do when buying a television set. Admittedly, because the process is much more complicated and requires more knowledge, the vast majority of homebuyers work with a professional. However, this doesn't necessarily remove the obstacles or protect us from financial or physical injury. Your home purchase will likely be the most important transaction of your lifetime. The results of that decision are generally long term, good or bad. The following examples are situations that have gone bad, even though a professional was involved. The rest of this book is designed to help you make your transaction a positive one with long-term benefits.

Roof Leaks Don't Lie

Several years ago, before Ken was a Realtor®, he was a private investigator. He received a call from an attorney who represented the Gordons, a couple who had recently bought a great old Hilltop home. Hilltop has always been a popular "moving up" area of Denver and is known for a certain degree of wealth and status, though the residences there are not ostentatious.

It seems the Gordons, during the moving-in process, filled the garage with dozens of boxes, many of which contained an old and rare-book collection they had been adding to for many years. The first weekend after they had moved in, before they finished unpacking, there was a rainstorm. Colorado is known for its summer "gully washers," rain storms that may last for only half an hour to an hour but dump tremendous amounts of rain and literally "wash out" the gullies, curbs and drainage systems. This was a true gully washer.

The Gordons never anticipated what would happen during that storm. It rained inside the garage, destroying a significant amount of their rare-book collection along with lots of other household items. The Gordons were away at the time, so the situation progressed unimpeded. The Gordons were devastated when they returned home.

Of course they had a professional home inspection when they were under contract to purchase the home, and the inspector did not indicate the presence of any roof leaks. They contacted their agent, who had recommended the home inspector, and asked for assistance. She contacted the sellers' agent, who professed no knowledge, then purportedly contacted the sellers, who also claimed innocence. The Gordons, in their extreme frustration, hired an attorney, who contacted Ken to conduct a thorough investigation.

The resulting lawsuit named several people: the sellers, the sellers' agent, the home inspector, the buyers' agent, and the two brokers, and here is why each was culpable.

The Sellers

Ken's investigation revealed that the sellers had experienced roof leaks as a matter of course for several years.

It was a Spanish-style tile roof and very expensive to repair or replace. He had located the roofing company that had performed repairs to the roof through the years. Ken obtained a statement from the owner of the company that, two years prior to the sale, he had told the sellers that he refused to do any more repairs to the roof because the patchwork was not working. The roof needed to be replaced. That disclosure to the sellers was also in writing from the roofing company. The Sellers' Property Disclosure, given to the buyers during the contract period, indicated that the roof was sound and had no leaks.

The Sellers' Agent

The sellers' agent was well known. She had been in business for many years and had a reputation for specializing in high-end listings in Cherry Creek, Hilltop, Mayfair and surrounding subdivisions in east Denver. She was also known for "dressing up" her listings so that they would sell quicker. That is, she would instruct her sellers to paint and do other cosmetic work to make the house look its best, and she would even lend expensive furniture when it would help make the home look luxurious. When Ken met with her and her broker, she denied any knowledge of roof leaks or other problems pertaining to the house. Ken was able to determine she instructed the sellers to paint parts of the interior of the home. He later learned from other sources she had specifically noticed water stains on living room, dining room and other walls and ordered those walls painted so the water stains would not be noticed by visiting prospective buyers.

The Home Inspector

Before meeting with the original home inspector, Ken hired another, and they had gone through the home in some detail. Among other things, they noted that in the attic, the sellers had placed sheets of plastic, each of which showed dried water marks. It was clear that the sheets of plastic were meant to capture water leaking from the roof. When Ken interviewed the home inspector, he admitted that he had never gone into the attic (even to inspect the insulation). He also admitted he had no money and no insurance and didn't even own a home. He said, "So sue me. I'll just go out of business." In fact, he was not bonded or insured and didn't even have any formal training, such as certification through the American Society of Home Inspectors or a similar organization.

The Buyers' Agent

Of all the parties, this lady was the most innocent. She truly felt she had done her job and was straightforward in her interview with Ken. She was also fairly new in the business, with a little more than a year of experience at the time she worked with the Gordons. However, she had made a serious mistake. She had recommended a home inspector without having checked out his credentials or reputation, and without even verifying that he was bonded and/or insured. The simple action of checking with her broker or other agents in her office to make sure her buyers had a truly professional inspector would have prevented this entire incident despite the efforts on the parts of the sellers and their agents to hide the evidence.

The Brokers

Regardless of the direct liability and culpability of the agents involved, they work for and are under the supervision of their brokers. In both cases, the brokers either failed to train their agents properly or failed to supervise their actions effectively. Hence, they were named in the lawsuit as well.

The Result

The Gordons won their lawsuit. However, it took more than a year, and in the meantime they had to finance a complete roof replacement on their own. It was also difficult to accurately ascertain the value of the rare books they lost, so the amount they collected for lost goods was far less than what they felt they should have gotten. Of course they received no compensation for the psychological pain and suffering they endured, nor for the time lost from work pursuing the lawsuit. So, in spite of the fact that some justice was eventually served, no one came out a true winner, and the entire mess could have been avoided with good representation and a little dose of honesty.

The Telltale Garbage

A few years ago, Ken's friends, the Crandalls, were moving back to Colorado and told him they were looking for a home in another town. Ken didn't sell real estate in that area, so he offered to refer them to a Realtor® who would represent their best interests. However, they said they had already gotten a referral from another friend and had met with that agent whom we'll call Jeremy. Ken simply recommended ways they could check out Jeremy's history and reputation and suggested they insist that Jeremy enter into a buyer-agency contract with them so they would be legally represented. This contract was especially important because they would be engaging in a home purchase at a long distance from their current home on the East Coast.

Well, you can give people advice with good intentions, but then it's up to them to take it. People don't like to have advice forced on them. The next time Ken spoke with the Crandalls, it was a few months after the sale had closed. They moved into their new home and had invited him to dinner. They spent most of the evening complaining about the problems they had to endure in the real estate transaction.

It appears Jeremy, their agent, was virtually non-existent from the time they went under contract until closing. It also turns out that he had sold the Crandalls his own listing and represented the seller in the transaction. He had refused to enter into a contract to represent the buyers because he said it was "against company policy," and the Crandalls did not press the issue. Jeremy did recommend a home inspector, and on one of her trips to Colorado, Alice Crandall met with the inspector to go through the house, but Jeremy did not attend the inspection. There were a number of items that needed to be repaired, including a failing heating system, and after returning home, Alice wrote Jeremy asking him to request the sellers make the repairs.

The response from the sellers was that a number of the items would be taken care of prior to closing. The Crandalls left the responsibility of overseeing those items to their "trusted" agent.

The Crandalls arrived in Colorado on the day of the closing. Before arriving at the closing, however, they drove by the house. In the driveway, directly in front of the garage, there was a huge pile of garbage, equivalent to two or three pick-up truck loads. The Crandalls were shocked and told Ken they had a sense of foreboding about the transaction, but they still didn't know what they were in for.

At the closing, they learned the sellers had come earlier and signed the closing documents. According to Jeremy, it was because they were completing the cleanup of the home and hauling away the offending garbage before they left town. They had people scheduled to assist and that made it necessary for them to sign early. Jeremy told them, "Everything has been taken care of. It's all right." Feeling somewhat reassured, the Crandalls went through with the closing, got the keys and drove to their new home.

You've probably guessed that the pile of garbage was untouched, and the sellers were not around. It was clear they had packed up and left. The garbage would be left for the Crandalls to deal with. Then they went inside. Two *small* items, the stove and refrigerator, which according to the contract were to remain in the house, had been removed. The heating system and several of the inspection items had not been repaired, and to add insult to injury, the house had not been cleaned at all.

Attempts to get Jeremy to respond were fruitless. It was suggested they had some recourse by filing a complaint with both the Association of Realtors® and with the Real Estate Commission. But the Crandalls eventually took the route of least resistance: cleaned up, performed their own repairs, replaced the missing appliances and went on with their lives.

Unfortunately, most unsatisfactory transactions end up the same way, with no one held accountable, no complaints filed, and buyers left with bitter memories and a resolution to not let it happen next time.

Part One

The Home-Buying Process: A Brief History

1. A Scenario Under the Old Rules

Rick, we thought you did an outstanding job as our buyer broker. We spent many useful hours with the customized booklets that you prepared. We were particularly impressed by the research that you did on the property that we eventually purchased. You found pertinent agreements with the homeowners association, you found errors in documents from the title company and you patiently explained the risks associated with water availability and mineral rights.

—Mike Brittingham and Kory Williams

In the past, if you wanted to buy a house in most parts of the country, you might respond to an ad, meet with a real estate salesperson, see their listing, and if that didn't work out, look at more homes.

Perhaps you would spend two or three days together looking at homes before you walked into that perfect property. During that time, you and "your" real estate salesperson became friendly, told jokes, shared stories, and probably had a meal or two together. When it was time to make the purchase, you knew you were working with a friend, and you got the distinct feeling that the salesperson was working for you.

You were wrong!

In those days, the law of the land as far as real estate transactions were concerned was called "the law of sub-agency." Under the law of sub-agency, that salesperson (with very few exceptions) worked for the seller and had an obligation to try to get the **seller** the best deal possible.

The agent's only obligation to you was to provide information you may have requested about the house, the neighborhood and so forth. If you didn't think to ask to see how much other homes had sold for in the neighborhood, the agent wouldn't have to show you. They were always obligated under state law to let you know of any material defects in the house they were aware of (for example, if it was located on expansive soils and had a constant problem with the foundation cracking). But rarely, if ever, did they recommend ways for you to benefit during the sale, such as getting the seller to pay your closing costs or helping you with other financing options.

The bottom line was that **you were on your own!**

2. Why Sellers Always Got the Best Deal

> Over the past three years, you have represented us in two purchases and one sale. You even helped in the sale of some property in another area. Your advice has always been insightful, honest and to the point. From our first purchase, a tiny condominium, we have gradually moved up to where we are now, in a detached home with plenty of room and great views. We can't imagine buying a home without a buyer's representative and we very much appreciate your participation in our efforts.
>
> —Leslie Day and John Burnette

Here is how the law of sub-agency worked. It was essentially established when real estate brokers began to share their listings. For years, the only way such brokers could sell a house was to contact everyone they knew and to advertise. A home seller would then try to identify a broker who knew the most people or was really effective at advertising. It was often like finding a needle in a haystack.

Broker associations were usually not very well organized, and even state laws governing real estate sales were, in many cases, somewhat primitive. Occasionally, one or more brokers would get together over a meal or coffee and share their listings. They might make a handshake agreement that if one of them brought in a buyer for another's listing, the commission would be shared.

Then, some years ago, enterprising Realtors® with the National Association of REALTORS® decided it would be beneficial to formalize the sharing of listings. This would benefit not only the Realtors® but the sellers as well. By implication, buyers would also benefit. This was the genesis of the **Multiple Listing Service** systems (the MLS).

With the advent of the MLS, all Realtors® who wanted to participate would put all of their listings in a central database, which usually resulted in a book issued periodically, that any Realtor® could peruse. Participation resulted in several things:

1. Over the last twenty years, as a matter of law, licensees represented the seller unless they had a written letter or a contract to the contrary.

2. Only a few buyer brokers had any sort of writing to the contrary, so it was a market full of seller agents.

3. Most Realtors®, as a result, ended up representing the seller even if the property was listed by another Realtor®.

This last point is very important. It makes clear that Realtors® almost always saw themselves as representatives of sellers. It was their mission in life, and they pursued it with a zeal unequaled in many professions.

Even though many Real Estate Commissions across the country required real estate licensees to disclose to a buyer they represented the seller, it was rarely disclosed.

Generally, they would tell the seller anything they learned about you, including your ability to pay more, your willingness to pay more, and your motivations for making the purchase.

You might feel certain you were working with a friend when you looked at those homes, but the bottom line was they were always representing the seller—and keeping you in the dark about it. More often than not, you were betrayed!

When you were ready to make the offer, you would typically ask "your" agent something like, "How low of an offer do you think the seller would accept?" They could legally only answer, "I'll submit whatever offer you want to make." You had to figure it out for yourself.

And when "your" friendly agent presented the offer? The seller might say, "Well, the offer seems pretty low. How high do you think they will go?" The agent might respond, "Well, they told me they wouldn't go over $100,000." And the seller would say, "Good, let's counter at that." As a result, lots of buyers paid more for homes than they had to. Perhaps you were one of them.

3. How the Rules Started Changing

You have provided services as a buyer agent for several of my real estate transactions. In each instance, you represented my interests well. I confirmed my first purchase without seeing it, based on videotape you took of the property and furnished to me. When I moved here, I saw the home for the first time, and it confirmed that we made a perfect choice for my needs. I subsequently purchased a prime investment property because of your exceptional diligence. A facsimile announcement of the property's availability was sent to your office about 5 p.m., and I was able to submit a contract within two hours. I don't know of another attorney who would have as much faith in another professional as I have had in you. I am extremely pleased with every transaction I have completed with you.

—Dee Phelps

Now, it is important to know this one-sided negotiating did not all happen in a vacuum. Buyers and sellers who felt cheated or defrauded complained, legislatures responded with tougher laws, and state regulatory agencies became more and more involved in the oversight of real estate practices.

The federal government also heard the cries. In 1983, the Federal Trade Commission (FTC) conducted a national survey of recent buyers of real estate to determine how they felt about their transactions. The results were nothing short of astounding. The FTC survey found that approximately two-thirds of all buyers surveyed thought they were being represented in the transaction when, in fact, they were not.

It became agonizingly clear that the lack of disclosure to buyers about the process was having a negative effect on the reputation of the real estate profession as a whole. Buyers were losing faith in the process, and with good reason. They were getting trod upon, taken advantage of, and in many cases, harmed financially. Lawsuits were being filed by consumers across the country against real estate licensees.

To their credit, there were many in the profession who did not feel the existing process was fair. Realtors® were beginning to realize the importance of representing buyers and developed contracts to do just that.

Buyer agency sprung from the determination of a small number of independent thinking, gutsy and radical Realtors®. With a contract in hand to represent a buyer, they would peruse the MLS, show properties, and make offers. Those offers started changing substantially from the norm. They would often include concessions from the seller: closing costs, financing points, lower prices, carpet and fix-up allowances, and other items paid by the seller on behalf of the buyer.

Traditional seller's agents began to take notice, and those who strongly supported the status quo often fought buyer's agents. They would present the offer then often create animosity in the negotiation process but let it go to contract. Then, at closing, they would keep all the commissions and refuse to compensate the buyer's Realtor®.

Many Realtors® operating as buyer's agents had to plead their cases in arbitration through the state Realtor® association or take the case to court in order to collect their fair share of the commission (called the cooperative fee split).

The National Association of REALTORS® discussions often became heated between traditionalists who didn't want to see the rules change and new-thinking, progressive Realtors® who felt change was necessary. The profession of real estate was evolving. But, as with anything that encompasses hundreds of thousands of members, and hundreds of local, state and national associations, it was experiencing a great deal of conflict in the process.

Many associations of Realtors® across the country recognized the importance of the discussion and joined with their Real Estate Commissions to research the issues. In many states, when legislation was introduced to change agency laws, it was supported by both the Association and the Commission. There are still a few states struggling with this issue.

Part Two

A New Law for the People

4. What Is Agency, Anyway?

We learned a lot about buyer agency working with you. When you showed us everything in the county in our price range, and we couldn't find anything we liked, that didn't stop you. You found us a home that was not listed, was not being advertised, and that even the owner didn't know he was going to sell. But it went together so easily. Even when we were back home in California getting ready for the move, you took care of the details. Then you helped introduce us to people in our new community and supported us in our new career. You are the best!

—Larry and Lorrie Keen

An Obligation Conferred

First of all, it is important to understand agency. It's easy to banter about words like *sub-agency* and *real estate agency*, but the fact of the matter is that *agency* is a legal term. Its use confers a legal obligation and some legal liability.

Let's say, for example, your parents are going to be away on a vacation for an extended period of time. While they are gone, they want someone to deposit their checks, pay their bills and carry on business for them as usual. What they want, in fact, is someone to keep their best interests in mind and to act accordingly. They ask you to represent them, to handle all the paperwork for them in their absence. In order for you to perform those functions for them legally, they would have to sign a document giving you power to act for them in those matters.

This document is called a *power of attorney*, and it makes you their *agent*, or their legal representative.

If you were to call your parent's banker in their absence and ask the banker to transfer money from one account to another, the banker would refuse—unless you can prove you are the *agent* of your parents. In order to do that, you would have to provide their banker with a copy of the power of attorney.

It is also important to understand that the person empowered to be an agent is often in a better position to handle their client's business than the client is. The *agent* is either physically in a better location to handle business for the client, or the agent is more knowledgeable about the matters to be handled than the client is. You hire an attorney—and the attorney becomes your agent—because the attorney understands law and you do not.

Sub-Agency

The same is true when working with real estate professionals. In the past, when Realtors® almost always represented sellers, they were the *agents* of those sellers, and other Realtors® they "hired" through the MLS became the sellers' *sub-agents*. As a consequence, all of the real estate salespeople involved had a legal obligation to represent the best interests of the seller in every transaction. Now, it could be argued that they also had an obligation to be honest with buyers, to disclose their relationship with sellers, but we believe most agents felt this might compromise the interests of the seller, justifying their silence.

So, buyers of real estate in the era of *sub-agency* were at a disadvantage, not because they were dealing with lying or unscrupulous agents, but because the rules were made with sellers in mind, and the sellers were always represented. But we should never lose sight of the fact that real estate professionals have always felt that, in order to be successful, they had to take listings (list properties for sale under contracts with sellers)—and the one with the most listings won. Every property listing they took made them an agent of that seller, and every action they took in the process of marketing the seller's home had to keep the seller's interests in mind. Is it any surprise buyers felt cheated?

Vicarious Liability

There is one other aspect of agency that merits discussion, and that is the existence of *vicarious liability*. Most people understand a liability is a risk; it's an exposure. You take on a liability when you hire an attorney to take actions on your behalf. If that attorney signs a contract on your behalf that creates an unattractive obligation to a third party, you are still liable for your attorney's actions. Your child could damage the property of another, and you might be held responsible for reparations. That is *vicarious liability*. It is extending your risk through reliance on, or responsibility for, others.

Every time you engage an agent to represent you, you take on some vicarious liability. (Remember the buyer whose agent recommended an uninsured home inspector? The buyer paid the price.) You rely on your agent to make decisions and recommendations on your behalf that are in your best interest. You have also engaged that agent because you believe their knowledge in this area is greater than yours and, you hope, greater than others in the same field.

Many lawsuits have been filed against agents by their clients for failure to act in a professional or prudent manner, or for otherwise putting the client unnecessarily at risk. When a client suffers a loss as a result of the agent's actions, that client will usually feel a need to be compensated for that loss. However, lawsuits are expensive, and many who have suffered losses do not file complaints.

Historically, the vast majority of lawsuits filed have involved seller's agents. There are so many ways a seller's agent can misrepresent a property and obligate a seller for the agent's misrepresentations. However, there are very few instances when a buyer's agent can misrepresent a buyer such that the buyer is put at risk. Nevertheless, even when retaining a Realtor® to represent you as your buyer's agent, you need to be aware there may be some vicarious liability. It will behoove you to ensure your agent is experienced, knowledgeable, professional, and willing and able to work for you.

What the Heck Is a Fiduciary?

Fiduciary is defined by the Random House Dictionary as "a person to whom property is entrusted for the benefit of another." So how does this fit into a book on real estate? Realtors® are agents who provide "fiduciary duties" to clients. They are entrusted with handling a real estate transaction with a level of care as though the property were their own. However, it seems most real estate agents never really understood what the word meant in terms of daily professional conduct. The industry position was that an agent represented the seller unless there was a written contract to the contrary. The buyers believed they were working with an agent who was "their agent" and owed them all the normal duties of loyalty and confidentiality.

As an industry perception, agents felt that when buyers said they were betrayed it was because the buyers were complainers. The fact was that real estate agents represented the seller at all times and generally treated the situation with this thought in mind: "Let's quit talking about professional responsibility stuff. Get the sale done and make some money." This attitude seemed to prevail in the real estate community. In the next chapter we will discuss a couple of events that provided the wake up call to real estate agents. Here we present the basic descriptions of agency.

Single Agency

With the changes in the laws governing real estate, many states created a term, called *single agency*. Under *single agency*, a seller could be represented by one real estate salesperson (*agent*), and a buyer could be represented by another real estate salesperson (*agent*). Some balance was potentially brought to the transaction. We say potentially, because many real estate salespeople around the country had to learn new rules. Some agents made the transition easily and happily and some did not. There was, and still is, some resistance in the real estate community to buyer's agents, but it is diminishing over time. Transactions are becoming less adversarial, and both buyers and sellers are feeling more fairness in the deals they make.

By far the most important aspect of these new laws is how they fleshed out and defined the single agency relationship. Generally, they established some procedures and indicators by which one could tell if the relationship was there. Single agency is a procedure whereby a single agent could represent a buyer or tenant and another single agent could represent a seller or landlord, each with their own obligations. Buyer agents are to:

- exercise reasonable skill and care on behalf of the buyer;

- promote the buyer's interests with the utmost good faith, loyalty and fidelity;

- disclose to the buyer any known adverse material defects of any property that the buyer intends to purchase;

- counsel the buyer as to those benefits and risks of the transaction actually known to the broker;

- advise the buyer to seek expert assistance where needed;

- account in a timely manner for money and property; and

- inform the buyer of the exposure to vicarious liability for the acts and omissions of agents working on the buyer's behalf.

Single agency laws require buyers to be informed consumers. It remains to be seen how well it works in practice.

Dual Agency

This is not a new term, but its use poses a hurdle many feel is impossible to overcome. While the practice of dual agency was abolished in Colorado effective January 1, 2003, it is still practiced in many other states. Dual agency exists whenever the same real estate firm represents both the buyer and seller in the same transaction. It requires the broker to simultaneously be an agent for and advocate for both the buyer and seller in the same transaction. This can obviously create conflicting allegiances. When an agent with one realty company represents a seller and an agent in another company represents a buyer, there's little conflict. When you sign a contract, you are retaining the agent's entire company to represent you in your purchase or sale.

Opponents of dual agency believe consumers are the losers in these situations, and it appears they may be. Think about it for a moment: You carefully retain the best agent in your marketplace to assist you in your home purchase. You select this agent to advocate for your interest in the transaction. Your agent assists in locating the perfect house, and now is the time when you really need their help. You've got questions on price, terms, inspections, seller accountabilities, due diligence, finance options, risks, competing buyers, neighborhood information, and more. Most of all, you want the transaction arranged to benefit you on all the negotiated issues.

However, the seller is also represented by the same agent or agency, and the agency has those same duties to be an advocate for the seller's benefit. How can the agency serve two masters? Consider just the issue of price alone. How is your agency going to argue for your *lower* price objectives and the seller's *higher* price objectives at the same time? What would your advice sound like from your agent when you are the buyer? Would it be, "At $200,000, this house is priced high. I wouldn't offer more than $170,000 for it." And then, when presenting the offer to the seller, for whom the agent is also to advocate on behalf of, they say, "This offer is ridiculously low. I'd counter around $195,000." Seems rather ridiculous, doesn't it? It's like the humorous Monty Python skit in which a man both pressed charges and defended himself in court for assaulting himself.

What would more likely happen is the agent would give no advice to either side and simply say, "You decide." Suppose the broker thought of the seller as an old friend and thought of the buyer as a stranger. Where would that leave the buyer? Recognizing this, the dual agent has the responsibility not to disclose to either party without the prior consent of the other the following issues: (1) Whether the buyer may pay more or the seller may take less; (2) the motivating factors for either party;

(3) whether the buyer or seller would agree to different financial terms; (4) any facts or suspicions about circumstances that potentially represent a psychological stigma on the property, and (5) any material information about the other party, unless non-disclosure would constitute fraud or dishonest dealing.

There Are Advantages to Dual Agency

As much as we feel dual agency is harmful to consumers, it does have some advantages. If you are dealing with only one firm, and especially if there is only one individual agent involved, your lines of communication are shorter. For example, if you ask your agent a question that requires input from the other party, you are likely to get a faster answer since there is one less firm in the chain of communication.

Another advantage may be one of motivation. If one firm is earning both sides of the commission they are more motivated to do what they can to make the transaction close if a major obstacle surfaces. This is to your benefit, unless the obstacle was your desire to cancel the transaction.

To protect yourself, discuss the firm's agency policy in your initial contact with them. Ask them to explain how they prevent dual agency from occurring. Of course, the agent you choose will also have to be experienced and competent in the rest of the skills needed to serve you, which we will address in other areas of this book.

Non-Agency

Some states have embraced an alternative to dual agency: non-agency. In a non-agency relationship, the firm has no fiduciary responsibilities to anyone. This arrangement is not attractive to consumers for the obvious reason: There are very few circumstances in which you would hire a firm that has no responsibility to you, and possibly no liability if they damage you.

Transaction Brokerage

Some states have adopted a completely new concept called transaction brokerage. It provides a radical and sometimes workable method of handling in-house transactions. Generally, it is described as a broker who assists one or more parties throughout a contemplated real estate transaction with communication, advisement, negotiation, contract terms and the closing of such transaction without being an agent or advocate for the interests of either party.

Transaction brokerage requires both parties to step back from the agency relationship to neutrality. The arrangement can make an in-house transaction work. Your agent can show you properties that fit your needs, desires and financial abilities. If an in-house listing fits, it should be shown to you. If you want to purchase that property, your agent lets you determine how to construct the offer and simply carries it back and forth between you and the seller until the two of you reach an agreement. The same neutral attitude is carried through each step of the process until the sale is closed.

In the real world, this may be carried too far. Any buyer who decides not to enter into a buyer-agency contract automatically is creating a transaction brokerage arrangement. That agent is obligated to be neutral, and while they can provide factual information regarding the properties you see, they are NOT your agent and cannot advocate for you. They are limited by your instructions in the professional advice they can give. If you are not completely familiar with real estate transactions, contracts and other documents, and if you do not know the market thoroughly, you need to recognize that *this relationship can be a serious detriment to your ability to strike the best deal*—especially when you are relying on the broker's knowledge of the market.

Joe King, a Denver attorney, has a practice that focuses on the defense of real estate agents. He says transaction brokers are sued more than any other type of agent. It appears a transaction broker tends to fall into the same trap that is used to catch sub-agents: They appear to be your friend and will act as a buyer agent. Then, when the chips are down, and you don't feel you were properly represented, they try to point out they were only a transaction broker.

Under a buyer-agent contract, the Realtor® has an obligation to insure your needs are met. There is an obligation to be sure you see all the properties available, which meet your parameters, until you've made a decision to buy. They can advise you whether particular issues are good or bad for you, which a transaction broker typically cannot.

Transaction brokerage was touted as a realistic method of filling the gap between what became the outmoded concept of sub-agency and the straight buyer agency. It was also recognized as a viable alternative to dual agency and the legal dilemmas posed by that relationship for in-house transactions. Since January 1, 2003, the use of transaction brokerage in Colorado has been significantly limited, particularly when you are working with a Buyer's Agent. But these changes can be better understood once you have read the following section on in-house transactions and designated brokerage.

In-House Transactions and Designated Brokerage

There are various ways to handle in-house transactions. There are some brokerage firms that only represent buyers; they never take a listing. Their belief is that they are the truest buyer representatives and that their business is uncluttered with seller representation. That may be true, unless you believe the individual is more important than the company. While a real estate salesperson must work within the philosophy and policies of their brokerage, an agent who meets all the criteria discussed in the previous chapter will serve you well regardless of what company they work for or the policies by which they are bound.

After you have purchased your home, you may also decide in the future to sell it. Naturally, if you had a good experience with your agent in the purchase, you would want to consider the same person to help you sell your house. So it's always good to keep your options open. Ultimately, you get to decide what is more important—the agent or the company's philosophy.

If your agent also takes listings, they will want to show you any of those listings that fit your parameters. If they didn't do so, you might be upset later when you discover you never got to see what might have been the perfect home. When your Realtor® shows you a home where they represent the seller, your relationship with them reverts to Transaction Brokerage.

Effective January 1, 2003, a dramatic change in agency law was adopted in Colorado. First, as discussed earlier, the concepts of Dual Agency and Sub-agency were abolished. But, more importantly, a new concept called Designated Brokerage has emerged, which promises to provide great benefits to both buyers and sellers. The difference is in how in-house transactions are going to be handled.

Ken served on the Designated Brokerage Committee for the Colorado Association of Realtors®, which had the task of drafting the language for the legislation. He worked closely with the Real Estate Commission, which had been advocating for this change for the past two to three years.

Until this change, if your Realtor® was your Buyer Agent, and you decided to purchase a property listed by the firm for which your Realtor® worked, your Realtor® had to switch you to a Transaction Brokerage relationship. Instead of advocating for you, they were required to be neutral, both for you and for the seller. This occurred even though your Realtor® may not have known or been acquainted with the seller, and in some cases, may not have even known the other Realtor® within the firm (some larger firms are constantly recruiting new agents). So, even though your Realtor® had a GENUINE allegiance to you, and none to the other side, they could not legally act on that allegiance. The reason for this logic was that the employing broker basically "owned" the property listings and, hence, the brokerage relationship with each buyer or seller rested with them. Your agent was basically a sub-agent of the employing broker.

Under Designated Brokerage, the agency relationship stops with your Realtor®. The employing broker has no agency relationship with any buyer or seller except for those with whom they are personally working. While they remain responsible for administrative oversight of all transactions, their Realtors® are free to represent their buyers and sellers as designated by them. That is, the employing broker has both the authority and the responsibility of designating in writing that your Realtor® can represent you, and another of their agents can represent the seller in the same transaction. Hence, even on an in-house transaction, your Realtor® can remain loyal to, and advocate for you.

This is true for all firms except single agent firms (independent brokers). In those cases, you actually have one person working with both the seller and the buyer. In this case, the law requires that the Realtor® must revert to transaction brokerage and be neutral for both parties. This is also the case with an in-house transaction where you choose to buy a property listed individually by your Realtor®.

We always felt constrained when our buyers wanted to purchase a property listed by another agent in our firm. Our natural instincts have always been to continue to advocate for our buyers, even if that meant taking advantage of a seller whom we did not know and felt no allegiance to. However, the law prevented us from continuing that agency relationship with our buyers. Now, the winner with the new legislation is you! You can continue to be represented. Nothing changes, unless it's our personal listing. And you win!

Compensation

Commissions in this country have historically been paid out of the proceeds of the sale, so it has been presumed that the seller is actually paying those commissions, thus setting up the argument the agent is working for the seller. Take a look: The sellers list their home, and in the listing contract they offer to pay some percent as a commission upon the successful sale of the home. The listing agent then offers a portion of that amount to any other real estate agent who brings in the buyer. The seller signed the listing contract in which the commission obligation was created.

Because the seller was presumed to be paying the commission, the argument was anyone receiving all or part of that commission was working for the seller. However, there has been another argument. Because the buyer is the one actually bringing the money to the transaction, the buyer is paying the commission. This argument has generally been held by a minority within the profession.

New agency laws basically eliminated the arguments by stating any party to a transaction may pay any broker's compensation, and the payment will not create or terminate any agency relationship within that transaction. Payment of commissions to both buyer's and seller's agents could continue to be made as it always had—out of the proceeds of the sale—without creating any argument for agency. In the final analysis, home values are established in this country with real estate commissions factored in as part of the value. That is because home sales have been, and almost always are, handled by real estate agents, and the cost of that handling becomes part of the ultimate sales price and value of the home. Therefore, it becomes a moot point who pays the commission—it is simply part of the home value and paid out of the proceeds of the sale. Please be aware that listing commission amounts or percentages are negotiable, and the form of commission agreed to may vary as well. There is no "standard" or "normal" commission.

Part Three

Let's Get Started

5. Playing the Field or Getting Engaged

We can't say enough about working with you. You helped us buy our home from a long distance, then helped our son buy his first home and then buy a lot next to us. In every case, you helped with advice but without pushing us when we couldn't make up our minds. Then you helped us negotiate, recommended a top-notch lender, home inspector and so on. We have always felt you were more of a friend than 'just a Realtor®.' Thanks for being with us every step of the way.

—Bob and Jo Ann Clark

So you're ready to look for a home. Perhaps you've been looking already, sort of as a hobby. I've got one question for you. What Realtor® are you working with?

If you are like many homebuyers, particularly when it's their first time, you may have been calling on ads or for-sale signs, going to open houses, and talking to agents to whom you have been referred. But generally, you have avoided committing to one, usually on the basis that you don't want to be pressured, or you're "just not ready."

You may also have found you are not getting much follow-up from the Realtors® you have seen. Do you wonder why?

Well, it might be helpful to know how real estate agents work and how you can get the best results working with them. First, just like you, they have to work for a living. Even though it sometimes seems like they work for free, believe me, they don't.

The number of agents who fail in this business is astounding. Fewer than 20 percent hang in there for more than three years. Why? Because they find out how difficult it is to actually make money. It's a *very* competitive field. If they've been around for a few years, they've learned a few things. One of those things is how to identify someone who is *playing the field*. You know who we mean. It's the prospective buyer, spending a little time with several Realtors® but not committed to any and probably not committed to the process of buying a home. Many consumers treat buying real estate just like buying a car. They think if they can keep several brokers on a string wondering who is going to get the business, they can strike a better deal. Nothing could be farther from the truth.

The more competent, professional and successful a Realtor® becomes, the more business they have, and the more discriminating they are in how they spend their time. If you spend much time with someone you are not committed to, it will likely be with someone newer to the business or less skilled at negotiating and getting deals to close. This is often the person who is building their business, or who is otherwise counting on their next commission to pay bills. In other words, their motivation may be more to help themselves than to help you. There is nothing wrong with working with a new or less experienced broker, but you have to take the whole person into consideration. Enthusiasm, willingness to learn, and a positive attitude go a long way toward compensating for lack of experience. There is nothing wrong with that, as long as you are getting good service. But there is one simple way of ensuring the service you get is the best available: Make a decision.

That's all there is to it. You should first decide if you are serious about buying a home and then determine if you qualify to do so. You should then select a Realtor® and enter into an agreement to work with that person exclusively. It's like getting engaged but not married. Kind of scary, right? It means you are making a commitment to the process and to the person. But taking that step will produce much better results in the long run.

If you are working with one Realtor®, and they know you are not hopping around from one to another, that person will become as committed to you as you are to them. They will become "your" Realtor®, and they will be working for you. They will likely work to help you get qualified for financing, and when that "hot" property comes on the market, guess who they're going to call? Believe me, it won't be the person who happened to stop in for an hour last weekend. It will be the buyer to whom they are committed; it will be you. After all, they're *obligated* to bring to your attention any property they can find that fits your needs. If it's a great deal, all the better.

As Realtors®, we have all had occasion to work with people who spend a little time with us, then leave with a comment like, "Please call me when that little cabin in the woods becomes available." We know they have left the same message with half a dozen other agents, and they are the last ones we will call.

We've sold numerous properties where our buyer was the only person to see the house. We try to check new listings regularly, and also watch the classified ads in the newspaper for homes being sold by owners. Sometimes we see a property that is obviously underpriced, or perhaps it is "priced for a quick sale." It then becomes a game—get our buyer into the property before anyone else sees it, because we know it will go fast. We're off with a quick call to the buyer to let them know, "We've got one." We can usually write a contract that same day.

We don't get paid until we produce a sale. We've worked with some clients for years before they bought a home. They either needed to get their finances in order or couldn't find the right home. That's a long time to wait to get paid, but because they worked with us exclusively, and we knew they were committed to finding a home, we didn't mind how long it took. There is not a lot of loyalty in this business, and there are a lot of short term thinkers—people who will unknowingly lose thousands of future dollars to save a thousand today. You will find that two-way loyalty pays off. The key is selecting the right agent.

6. How to Select Your Realtor®—Credentials, History, Training and Attitude

We really would like to thank you for all your understanding and kindness you showed us in a difficult situation. You knew what a traumatic time it was for my family to be moving from an area we had been in and loved for over twenty years. Thank you for your professionalism, knowledge, honesty, energy, and above all else, kindness.

—Jeanne M. Brown

Credentials

You've probably noticed that when we've used the term *Realtor®* in this book, it is often capitalized and the registration mark is used. There is a reason for that. The term *Realtor®* is a trademark of the National Association of REALTORS® (NAR), and anyone who uses that term as part of their professional identity must be a member, not only of NAR but also of their state and local associations. Anyone who is not a member, but is legitimately working in the real estate profession, is still licensed by their state real estate commission and can be identified as an agent, a real estate salesperson, a real estate broker and so on.

When *Realtor®* is used however, it means several things. NAR members have training available only to members. They have the benefit of local meetings and state and national conferences where they can network with other Realtors®. Many deals are actually made for buyers and sellers at those events.

There is a price to pay: Members subscribe to a Code of Ethics, which commits them to conduct their business with a sense of fair play. The public has some recourse when they feel they have been lied to, mistreated, or cheated. They can file an ethics complaint with the local association requesting the Realtor® be disciplined, or request arbitration if they feel they have actually been cheated out of money. The Grievance Committee and the Professional Standards Committee of the organization handle these complaints. While a member is not bound to submit to the grievance process when a complaint is initiated by buyers or sellers, most do because it is a much simpler and less costly method of justice than going to court.

Members have to pay dues, and the MLS charges other fees to maintain a membership in good standing. Although some lawsuits have forced various Multiple Listing Services to allow access by non-Realtors®, many non-Realtors® still do not have the benefit of MLS access. The bottom line is that members are in a position to provide much better service to you than non-members. Those who do not have the Realtor® designation are operating independently, and they are often not doing enough business to justify the costs involved in belonging. A non-Realtor® may have a high level of ethics, but they are not bound by the same code of ethics that governs a Realtor®'s professional actions.

So for starters, get a Realtor®. You'll usually find the designation on their business cards.

History

If you were taking in a roommate or boarder, you would screen that person to see if you were compatible. If you were renting out property, you would take a rental application and check out the renter's references and credit history. If you were going into business with someone or hiring someone, you would be smart to conduct a background check. It never hurts to know who you are working with. The same is true with a real estate agent. In one survey of the National Association of REALTORS®, one-third of the respondents said they would not use the same agent for a purchase in the future. That is a high degree of dissatisfaction.

As consumers, we have a terrible history of picking professionals—doctors, lawyers and, yes, real estate agents. We get a referral from a friend, attend the appointment, and that's usually as far as we go. If we end up dissatisfied later, it's our own fault for not taking responsibility for our own selection. We need to prescreen, ask questions, get a feel for how compatible we might be and determine how well that professional can meet our needs.

It is sometimes difficult to avoid working with a friend in the business and to select someone else, but it might be the most valuable decision you could make. We have known people who listed their home with a friend who specialized in commercial sales and never sold a house. Maybe they were feeling sorry for them. You need to ask some questions before starting with any real estate agent. Don't sit down and say, "We're looking for a house in the $200,000 range." Try something like, "Before we start, I'd like to learn a few things about you." Interview your potential agent, ask questions, and determine the following important issues to your satisfaction.

Get a Full-Time Agent

Most full-time agents work 50-60 hours a week or more. They are committed to their work and to their clients. A part-time agent is there to make a deal when it comes along but either doesn't need the income a full-time career will produce, such as a retiree, or isn't making it yet (and may hold two or more jobs). Within reasonable limits, a Realtor® should fit their schedule to yours, not the other way around.

Questions to ask:

✓ What other type of work do you do?

✓ Do you work full time in real estate?

✓ How flexible is your schedule?

✓ How available are you to show properties on weekdays, weekends, mornings, evenings?

Get an Agent Who Is Busy

A successful Realtor® is busy and will not be able to spend all day, every day with you, but spending a couple of half-days a week to look at property is generally sufficient. Again, it depends on your circumstances. If you are only in town for two days, you might need their full attention while you are there, and you should ask for it.

Ask your potential agent how many sales (called sides) they closed last year and the year before. A "side" is one side of the sale. When one Realtor® had the listing and another one brought in the buyer, each produced one "side." An agent who has closed only four to eight sides in a year is not doing enough business to merit having yours. Either they need money, just got started, or can't get enough business to survive and they are on their way into another profession. An agent who has done 15 or 20 sides is not making a great deal of money but is surviving and probably growing, and believe it or not, they're far above the national average.

An agent who is doing 40-50 or more sides a year is very busy—usually for a reason. They have attracted business, hopefully because they have served people well, although some Realtors® generate lots of business simply through smart advertising. It is, therefore, important to get a sense of how many transactions were results of referrals from past clients.

Questions to ask:

✓ How many sides did you close last year?

✓ Is that usual for you?

✓ How many sides did you close the year before?

Make Sure the Broker Works Mostly With Buyers

If you are considering a real estate purchase, make it a top priority to select a Realtor® who has a history of working primarily with buyers. Now that you know how busy the agent is, ask how many of those sides were working with buyers and how many were listings. We suggest this ratio should be weighted two to one in favor of buyer representation. We'll talk more about credentials below, but if a Realtor® has the ABR designation (Accredited Buyer Representative), they have already taken training specific to buyer representation and have demonstrated a commitment to working with buyers.

Questions to ask:

✓ What percent of your business comes from representing buyers?

✓ How much of your business comes from referrals?

✓ Can I speak with several of your most recent buyers?

Check Out the Broker's Specialty

If you are looking for a home, select an agent who specializes in residential sales. If you want to buy an apartment building or a business, select someone who specializes in commercial sales. There are numerous specialties in real estate, and your agent's specialty should be consistent with your goals. Note that in larger metropolitan areas, Realtors® also tend to specialize in geographic areas, in price ranges, or with types of buyers. An agent who primarily sells million-dollar homes won't have the time for the $200,000 homebuyer. Some agents specialize in helping first-time homebuyers, while others really don't want the additional responsibility involved.

Questions to ask:

- ✓ Do you have a specialty?
- ✓ What are the price ranges of the homes you sell?
- ✓ What area/region do you specialize in?
- ✓ Do you sell commercial and residential real estate?

Make Sure the Broker Is Technologically Current

In today's world, it is becoming vitally important to work with professionals who are computer literate and have a grasp on some of the new gadgets designed to improve service to their customers. What does that mean?

First, many states require Realtors® to use certain forms in real estate transactions. These forms are almost always available on computer programs, and this presents the quickest, most accurate way to generate contracts. Those who continue to hand write their contracts, or who use a typewriter to fill in the blanks on standard forms are living in the past and are demonstrating an unwillingness to keep up with the times, and they may not be capable of providing the best service.

Other types of software allow Realtors® to track their customer's needs, access increasingly more sophisticated MLS systems, and communicate by email. Digital cameras allow photos to be sent by email to out-of-area buyers with information about new listings and hot properties, complete with interior and exterior views as part of the package.

At a minimum, if the real estate agent you are interviewing is not able to utilize a computer, beat a hasty retreat. Make sure when they say they're computerized, they're not just relying on an assistant or a shared secretary to do all the computer work for them. Where will you be if their assistant is not around or is too busy to prepare the contract? You could be waiting while a competing offer takes the property you want.

Questions to ask:

✓ Can I have your email address?

✓ What is the address of your website?

✓ Can you send me listings and photos by email?

✓ What forms do you typically download for use?

✓ What technology do you use in your business?

How Is a Mutual Commitment Established?

People who commit to work together usually put the agreement in writing. Ask the agent you are interviewing if they regularly enter into a buyer-agency contract. A good agent will generally not work with someone unless there is a mutual commitment—even if it's only for a very short time, enough to determine if you are compatible. That commitment can take the form of a written buyer-agency contract in which your agent agrees to represent you, and you agree to work exclusively with your agent. Or it could be an exclusive transaction broker contract, if you do not want representation.

There are Realtors® who will not show property to anyone who has not signed a buyer-agency agreement with them. However, they understand when they and a potential buyer have just met, they know very little about each other, and there is hesitation about signing a long-term commitment. So they will suggest an agreement be signed for one day only. At the end of the day, the buyer will either decide if they want to work with someone else (in which case the commitment is over), or they can't afford or don't want to buy in this market, or they want to continue working with this agent (at which time the agreement is extended, usually for several months).

See the next chapter on buyer-agency contracts for a more detailed discussion of this important issue.

Training

Anyone worth their salt in any profession continues to update their knowledge about the work they do. Doctors, lawyers and mechanics face an ever-changing world when it comes to their professions and must take classes to continue to be of service to their customers. The same is true of Realtors®.

State laws require continuing education, but the requirements are usually minimal: three or four one-day classes every two or three years. Good Realtors® find the time to take much more training than that. There are a number of designations denoting certain continuing education landmarks and they are often signified on business cards in the form of letters following their name. While some may be in areas not related to residential sales, all show a commitment on behalf of the Realtor® to keep their professional skills honed, and that's good. Do not work with someone who demonstrates no interest in continuing education. Look for some of the following designations on your prospective agent's business card.

ABR—Accredited Buyer Representative—requires additional training in agency issues and a thorough understanding of what it takes to represent buyers. While your Realtor® does not need this designation to represent buyers, it denotes their commitment to doing so. Graduates are members of the Real Estate Buyer Agency Council (REBAC) and receive continuing information to keep them informed of new buyer agency issues. While the numbers are growing, the percentage of Realtors® who have this designation is still low. When you find a Realtor® who is an ABR, talk to them. For buyers, it is more important than any other designation you will see below. It represents a commitment and a mindset oriented toward the buyer's best interest.

GRI—Graduate REALTORS® Institute—represents approximately 80 hours of advanced education beyond the training that is required to be licensed. It is usually the first step to becoming more informed and professional.

CRS—Certified Residential Specialist—requires completion of numerous two-to-three-day classes held around the country. It takes the average Realtor® a few years to complete and usually costs $5,000 to $10,000 in tuition and travel costs. It provides significantly increased and detailed knowledge in residential issues and is the graduate degree of residential sales. Graduates are members of the Residential Sales Council (RSC) and receive continuing information in a variety of ways to keep them abreast of new issues in this area.

ALC—Accredited Land Counselor—similar to the CRS, this usually requires several years and several thousand dollars in costs to achieve. It's the graduate degree in the area of land sales.

CCIM—Certified Commercial Investment Member—like the CRS, this is the designation for experts in commercial property sales, like shopping centers, industrial, office and apartment buildings. It requires extensive continuing education and graduates are members of the Commercial Sales Council.

e-PRO—Certified Internet Real Estate Professional—This is the only certification program of its kind recognized nationwide and endorsed by the National Association of REALTORS®. Those searching for a Realtor® can have confidence that e-PRO graduates are savvy with all aspects of the Internet. They not only take the Internet empowered consumer seriously, they are also able to meet their online needs.

Attitude

We just cannot end this section without a discussion about attitude and disposition. We mentioned a good, winning attitude makes up for a lot, and it's true. We'd much rather work with a newly licensed agent who really wants to help than some old curmudgeon who has been in the profession for years, thinks they know all the answers and will not listen to anything new. There are a lot of worn-out real estate agents who have "seen it all" still occupying desk space in offices across the land.

Your initial interview with a prospective agent will tell you a lot about their approach to life. Work with an optimist, not a pessimist. Listen to their answers to your questions. Are they saying, "There's nothing available in your price range." Or are they instead saying, "It might be difficult to find exactly what you want in that price range, but let's look at some properties so you have a better handle on this market."

It isn't brain surgery to figure this out; look for a good, positive attitude as part of your evaluation process.

7. The Buyer-Agency Contract

When making such an important purchase as real estate, we would insist that our broker/agent work for our best interests alone. You worked with us as our buyer agent and used your experience to find a house and negotiate the best deal for us in a tough resort market.

—Daniel and Julie Zangari

A buyer-agency contract is a contract between the buyer (you) and the Realtor®, and it works two ways. First, the Realtor® becomes your agent and is obligated to represent your best interests. Second, the contract represents your commitment to the Realtor® and says that you will work with them exclusively. This agreement means that when you see a sign on a property, you will not call the listing agent yourself to negotiate a deal, nor will you go into a property that is for-sale-by-owner to do the same. Instead, you will call your agent and ask them to get you information on the property. You now have an agent; use them. The whole purpose of this exercise is to get you the best deal possible. If you have selected a good agent, you should recognize they have the experience and the skills necessary to represent you effectively. It takes a modicum of trust to see that play out and it is now time for your Realtor® to earn their commission.

There are a few items you should pay particular attention to in a buyer-agency contract. In some states, most of these things are already part of the standard contract, but in many other states, this may not be the case. Before you sign, at least discuss the following topics:

Confidentiality

If you are to be represented effectively, it is imperative that the agent keep confidential any information they learn about you. In particular, the fact that you may be able or willing to pay more or accept concessions, and your motivating factors for the purchase should not be revealed, except as a valid negotiating tool with your prior consent.

In addition, you have a right to be assured that confidential information remains confidential even after you have bought your home or after your contract with the agent has expired or been terminated in any way. If you make an offer on an in-house transaction (where the seller is also represented by the brokerage that is representing you), information about you should remain just as confidential as when you are negotiating for a property listed by another firm. (Refer back to Chapter 4).

Scope of Work

The contract will contain a description of what type of property your agent is instructed to seek for you. Make sure the description fits your needs. If you are looking specifically for a residence, make sure the language limits the search to that. Do not accept language that says "any property." If you are considering purchasing a home from a family member or friend, you may ask to have that property excluded from the contract. However, you may want to ask your agent what they would charge to handle that transaction for you. Pitfalls can still exist and in fact can be more serious and more heart-wrenching when dealing with someone close to you. Many close relationships have been damaged or ruined when friends and relatives have done business together. It's usually not because of a lack of good intentions. It happens because objectivity is lost, personal feelings get exaggerated and hurt, and the process erodes. We've worked on numerous deals where family members and close friends were involved, and we have found that it becomes vitally important to ensure a win/win deal for everyone involved.

Compensation

Now is the time, not later, to determine how your agent gets paid. There are a variety of ways this can occur. You can agree to pay them a flat fee at closing, an hourly fee, a commission based on how much they save you from the listing price, or you can agree to any number of other strategies.

There is an option, however, which is generally accepted, and which most buyers find more acceptable than paying money out-of-pocket: Your agent gets paid out of the proceeds of the sale at closing. Keep in mind that the listing agent or broker is being paid a commission, which is described in the listing contract with the seller. The listing agent or broker then typically offers half of that commission to another agent who might bring in the buyer for the property. That compensation, called the "co-op" or cooperative fee split, is paid to your agent at closing. If you were to select one of the other compensation choices above, that co-op could be credited to you at closing.

If your real estate agent is to be paid at closing based on a percentage of the purchase price of the home, it is doubly important to have someone who you feel will put your best interests in front of their own.

What about for-sale-by-owner properties? The exact commission to be paid in those cases needs to be spelled out and written into the offer to purchase. When the contract is submitted to the owner, the commission is included in the discussion. There are times when a seller being represented by a Realtor® refuses to pay a buyer-agent. This occurrence is rare, but there are still brokers out there who look at buyer-agents as the enemy. In a case like this, you and your agent should have a discussion to determine how payment will work, or if it is even worth it for you to negotiate for that house. We usually include language in our buyer-agency contracts to accommodate this, and it would be wise to discuss this up front.

In any event, keep in mind that your agent, unlike most professionals who get retainers or charge by the hour, does not get paid until a property is closed (unless you have agreed to another arrangement). Every Realtor® works on transactions that never close, and they do not get paid for those. Also, home values across the country are established historically with a real estate commission included. That means a part of the purchase price is almost always paid to an agent for professional services. An appraisal of value does not separate one from the other.

Length of the Contract, Cancellation

Many buyer-agents typically write contracts for six months, which is a long time. Often we work with buyers of second homes, and the process involves communicating with them when they are in another city or state. We will coordinate property showings with their vacations to the area, and sometimes they buy properties we've recommended sight unseen. Even when working with locals, using a six-month representation period makes sense.

This long period can be scary. What if you decide you do not like your agent? What if your plans change? The simplest answer to this is to ask for a cancellation clause. Always include a clause that says either party, the buyer or agent, may cancel the contract for any reason whatsoever by providing written notice to the other party of that decision. While we might ask for a ten-day advance notice, we believe you can't force people to work together who are not compatible. If your Realtor® is willing to give you this "out" in your contract, you can bet they are fairly confident of their ability to represent you effectively. Keep in mind you would not be able to cancel a contract for a property on which you are already negotiating, and every contract will have what is called a "holdover" clause. That means if, after terminating the contract with your agent, you go back to a property you saw with that agent and buy it, they may be entitled to a commission.

The entire contract should be designed to be fair to both parties. It is fair to be able to cancel a contract when two people cannot work together. It is not fair to have someone do a lot of work for you and then cancel. You should be able to determine in the first or second meeting with your Realtor® whether or not you are compatible. Don't spend several weeks or months together and then decide to go with someone else.

Once the contract establishing the relationship between you and your Realtor® is complete, it's time to start looking for a home.

Part Four

Getting Your Home

8. Getting the Money

> The creative financing you recommended not only allowed us to qualify for more house than we thought we could afford, but will save us thousands in tax credits each year. Thanks for working with us so long. Your patience and willingness to work with us paid off.
>
> —Kent and Julie Brown

Real estate is such a great investment! There is probably nowhere else where you can leverage so much with so little. You can purchase a $100,000 home with $3,000. If that home goes up in value $10,000 (or 10%) in a year, you've more than tripled your $3,000 investment (333%). Sound too good to be true? It's not. People do it every day. The best place to start investing in life is in your personal residence. If you are renting—stop! Stop now! Renting is a losing proposition. All the money goes out and none comes back to you. If you own your home, you get the advantage of an appreciating asset (it grows in value), and you get the tax advantage of getting to deduct the interest portion of your payment. Ask your tax accountant about this, but for now let's talk about how to get the majority of the money to buy your home.

There are times when a parent, aunt or uncle will finance your home for you, but most people use a financial institution—the lender. The lender is probably the second most important member of your team after your Realtor®. Make sure you have a lender that specializes in providing loans for the type of purchase you are making. If you are buying a home, you will use a residential mortgage lender—the loan you obtain on your home is typically called a *mortgage*. If you are buying a business, you will need a commercial lender. If you are buying land, with certain exceptions, you will probably use a bank. A mortgage lender can do land loans if you are buying a lot and plan to build a home on it immediately. Many mortgage companies now offer what is called a "one-time close, construction-to-perm" loan, which will help you finance the land purchase, provide the construction financing, and then provide the permanent financing once the home is built.

There are three primary sources for financing your home purchase: banks and credit unions, mortgage bankers and mortgage brokers. Most people are aware that banks and credit unions loan money for a home purchase, including the former savings and loan associations. Banks, credit unions and S&Ls would lend money directly to you from their own pool of funds, usually based on customer deposits. A title used by the person you would actually work with at these institutions would be "loan officer." Loan officers are often paid a commission in addition to their salary. This is their incentive to get loan applications.

Mortgage bankers are also direct lenders and use their own funds, or those of wealthy investors, but they usually do not keep the loan. They will often sell off the loan to one of the government-sanctioned major home lenders like Freddie Mac or Fannie Mae. You might not know your loan was sold off because they often continue to service the loan by mailing your statements and collecting your payments. You would probably be working with a "loan officer" at a mortgage banking company also.

Mortgage brokers shop around for you, searching for the lender with the program or interest rate that fits your situation. They take your application and can use it to apply to dozens of lenders like banks and mortgage bankers as the intermediary between borrowers and lenders. They can't control interest rates or terms and are usually paid by the lender and/or from the points they charge.

The points you pay to buy your loan are often the same as going direct to the lender. One point equals one percent of the loan amount.

In all states, banks are regulated by various government agencies in their practice of providing home loans. However, in Colorado, mortgage lenders and mortgage brokers do not have to be licensed. This means anyone can get into the business, say they are a mortgage lender, do a lousy job for you, and you have no recourse through a licensing body. Even though many states require lenders to be licensed, lenders vary widely in honesty and integrity. Therefore, you still must be extra diligent in selecting your lender and your loan officer. They can hold the key to your purchase.

A loan officer is much like a real estate agent; you may be referred to one by a friend, may have a family member in the business, or happen to meet one by accident. Just remember that not all loan officers are alike. A good Realtor® will have a short list of lenders and loan officers who have proven they know what they are doing, only make promises they can keep, are known for not having last-minute surprises, have a substantial menu of loans to cover most situations, and whose rates and costs are competitive. You want to avoid last-minute surprises like finding out a day or two before you are supposed to close on your home purchase that the underwriter is requiring a list of conditions, which will be impossible to meet prior to closing, or is denying your loan.

Beware of the lenders who advertise the low rates in major newspapers or on the Internet. Purchasers have often started their loan applications before they met and retained a quality Realtor® to assist in their home purchases. In many of these cases where the clients stayed with that lender, they have regretted their selection. Typically, something goes wrong. The most common problems are interest rate increases, disregarding good faith estimates, hidden fees, processing delays, and lost documents.

We keep lists of lenders who meet our criteria, and a good Realtor® will also be familiar with the basics of loan processing and the types of loans available, so they can provide guidance as you work with the lender and can tell if the person you are working with is knowledgeable. However, many agents simply refer you to a lender and stay completely out of the process. We feel teamwork will get more deals done and we tend to stay involved and brainstorm unique possibilities with our buyers and their lenders.

Married or Not?

Ken worked with a young couple a few years ago who were attempting to purchase their first home. They were not married. The problem was Bob had impeccable credit but no cash in the bank. Jill had numerous credit problems in the past but had enough for the down payment and closing costs in the bank. In Ken's meeting with them and their lender, it was clear that Jill could not be on the loan. A condition of certain loans (in this case, it was an FHA loan) is if the borrower is to receive a gift of money from another party, that other party has to be a blood relative.

Under the circumstances, there was no way Jill could give the money to Bob for this home purchase, no matter how close their relationship was. Ken suggested one way to make this work; they could get married. The lender said, "Yes, that would work." The couple, looking a bit chagrined, said in fact they were planning to get married but not for another several months. Ken suggested, "Well, just don't tell anybody. Do it quietly at the courthouse, then have your ceremony with your friends when you had planned." That's exactly what they did, and they were in their new home when they got married. This couple, by the way, has since traded up twice to the home of their dreams.

Are Better Rates Real?

In a contrasting example, a recent first-time homebuyer, whom we'll call Jack, started out with a lender Ken had recommended. Then Jack read an ad placed in a major Denver newspaper by a lender who promised very low interest rates under a new program. Remember the earlier warning? Jack decided he wanted to switch his loan to the lender who advertised the low rates. The clients always have the right to choose their own lenders, but we will caution them when we are not familiar with a lender they choose. We cannot vouch for that lender's service, competence or knowledge. Often we interview the lender to try to determine the viability of the loan program they are offering and to get a sense of how well that lender can represent the client.

In this case, Ken confirmed that the loan program, while new, was legitimate. It was an adjustable rate loan, which started at a very low interest rate, then increased to market rate over time. There were some pitfalls to the loan, and he made sure Jack understood them. He made the lender send a good faith estimate and Jack decided to proceed. The lender was very positive about Jack's qualifications, and assured everyone this loan would be a "slam dunk." However, the lender could not get the loan processed in time, and they had to extend the contract once. Then, two days before the extended closing, the lender called Jack to tell him his loan had been denied then offered to switch him to another loan with a very high interest rate.

Jack called in horror, completely frustrated, and afraid he had lost his dream home. Ken had to do some fast negotiating to keep the deal together. Ken called the lender he first recommended, the one Jack had started with but dropped. She got Jack to provide them with a copy of all his paperwork, and in less than 48 hours, the lender Ken recommended got Jack complete and unconditional loan approval, and at conforming rates. While the seller was getting angry over the extensions, they were able to convince his listing agent that another short extension was better than seeking another offer on the house. The sale closed the following week and Jack is now a happy homeowner.

Prequalification and Preapproval

There is a significant difference between being prequalified for a loan versus being preapproved for the loan. The difference between them is like thinking you could afford to buy a home as opposed to having the bank say you actually qualify. A prequalification letter says you earn enough money to buy a certain priced home.

For a prequalification letter, the lender will check your credit, get basic information from you on your income and debts, and be able to tell you approximately how much of a mortgage you can qualify for. A preapproval letter could be issued after the lender has verified your information and actually run your loan application through the underwriting process. The approval would be subject to contract conditions and appraisal of the property.

If you were selling your home, who would you consider to be the stronger buyer: Someone with a preapproval letter or someone with a prequalification letter?

Many lenders are also able to perform what is called "desktop underwriting." If your credit is good enough, and if it appears your income and debt ratios will work, the lender can submit a loan application immediately by computer and then receive, almost immediately, an answer from the underwriter. Usually, it will come in the form of full loan approval up to a certain amount subject to an appraisal of value on the property, or with certain conditions that have to be met (such as verification of the information submitted).

If the lender's preapproval process does not allow you to buy a home, which you feel is suitable, you could ask about increasing your purchasing power by having your parents co-sign, by taking in partners, or by getting down payment assistance from friends, relatives or government programs. You could also ask if the lender has other non-traditional loan programs that would allow a higher purchase price. For example, there is a program that allows better rates for home purchases when the home meets certain requirements for energy efficiency.

Note that when you enter into a contract to purchase a home, there will be a deadline by which you must have full loan approval. If you do not obtain full loan approval by the contract deadline, you may terminate the contract. If you do not terminate the contract, you will be obligated to purchase the home or lose your earnest money deposit. Of course, that means you must be working with a lender you can trust, and you must be sure not to spend the money you will be required to bring to the closing table.

When you and your Realtor® have established your relationship with a mortgage lender and established your purchase limits, you can embark on a home search where you will only be looking at properties you can realistically afford.

The Good Faith Estimate

A good faith estimate is a form your lender provides you that shows several things. It shows the lender's regular charges, along with the other anticipated closing costs involved with the loan. It utilizes those figures to estimate the total amount of cash you will need to buy your house and calculates your approximate monthly payment. Some lenders will insist they cannot provide a good faith estimate until you have a property under contract or in escrow. That's baloney. Good faith estimates are simply that—estimates—and they can be prepared quickly and easily. In fact, some lenders we work with will prepare several, one for each loan scenario they are discussing with you. It assists you in comparing those loans so you can decide which one to take.

It also gives you something to compare with other lenders if you happen to be shopping for the best rates and costs. If one lender charges, for example, a $450 loan processing fee, and another charges $150, and the rates and other fees are the same, you might want to spend more time with the lender who charges less. But do not let these fees be the only reason for selecting a lender. Consider what happened to Jack. A good mortgage broker is worth their weight in gold.

You should also get a good faith estimate on two other occasions:(1) when you have a property under contract, and your Realtor® provides a copy of that contract to the lender; (2) when you change loan programs, either because you don't qualify for the one you started with, or you decide on a different plan. Once you are under contract, many of the items that were estimated on the first good faith estimate are known, so the *estimate* is more accurate and closer to reality.

The Last-Minute Fees

Occasionally, one of our clients decides to use a lender we haven't recommended. In one case, a couple decided to work with a lender who was renting a home from this couple's parents. The lender promised to cut his origination fee in half because of the relationship. Usually, a lender charges a 1.0% loan origination fee. That fee is generally split between the loan officer and the mortgage company he works for. In this case, the lender either gave up his portion of that fee, or he worked it out with his boss for the company to discount the deal. At any rate, when Ken compared his good faith estimate with other lenders, the reduced fee made the difference. Their loan was going to be about $140,000, so a 1.0% fee would have been $1,400. They saved $700 by going with this lender, all other things being equal.

Ken met with the lender and told him if he really took care of the clients, he would get other referrals from him. The lender was just getting established in the area, and he was eager for the new business. However, it took him longer to process the loan than he thought, and Ken did not have a settlement statement until the actual day of closing. Ken called him and the title company to bring something to their attention—the fact that there was a 1.0% loan origination fee on the statement rather than .5%—and asked for a correction. But this loan officer insisted he had met with the clients, and because they had not locked in their rates, and rates had gone up somewhat, he took a full origination fee rather than increase the rate.

Ken asked to see the new good faith estimate that he should have provided if this were true. He said he did not provide one, but the clients understood the new loan terms. The clients insisted there was no such agreement, and at the closing table they were faced with a dilemma. They had to close with the charges as they appeared, or get the lender to write them a check back for the .5% difference or walk away and refuse to close on the home. They closed, and did not get a refund from the lender. They were angry with him but happy to be in their new home. That lender has never received a referral from Ken, and within a few months he was out of business or at least gone from the area. He certainly does not rent from the clients' parents anymore.

Loan Types and Interest Rates

There are a variety of loan types available, and the loan program you select will depend first on your ability to qualify and then on your right to select one over another.

A starting place regarding your ability to qualify for a mortgage loan is the quality of your credit report. Every lender uses the FICO score, which stands for the company who created the scoring formula: Fair Isaac Company. They are a third party who provides the score to a potential lender. The lender does not calculate the score but uses it to establish a borrower's credit worthiness. Until recently, the components of this scoring system were kept secret, but it's been announced that consumers will be able to get information about their score at *www.fairisaac.com*. In general, they use different models and adjust the score depending on various factors, such as the amount of credit, the level of credit cards with no balances, cards with high balances, bankruptcy, payment patterns and so on.

At the current time, a score over 700 is excellent. Scores of 620 or above would normally allow you to qualify for A or A+ quality loans. These have the lowest interest rates and the most favorable terms. If we use mortgage rates of 7% as what would be the best available at the time, a person with scores in this range would qualify for that rate. Scores below 620 would normally put you in what is called a "sub-prime" category, also called "B" or "C" loans. The interest rate charged would depend on a variety of specific information on your credit report but could be as high at 14% in today's market. The rules vary considerably between lenders on sub-prime loans.

In addition to the money the borrower would pay for doing a credit check, getting title insurance, paying escrow charges and appraisal fees, there is also a cost to get most mortgage loans: *points*. Points refer to the cost of purchasing a loan. One point represents 1% of the loan balance. On a $100,000 loan this would be $1,000 to purchase the loan. If a credit score puts someone in the B or C range, the points could rise to 4, meaning it could cost up to $4,000 to purchase that loan. Other fees could rise from $275 to process the same paperwork for a typical A borrower, to $650 for a B or C borrower.

Certain loans are specially targeted for first-time homebuyers and offer features such as low down payment (as little as nothing down), competitive interest rates, and the ability to have a co-signer or receive down payment assistance from another source. There are so many loan variables that it would be impossible to discuss them all here.

At the time of this writing, second-home loans are available for 10% down with interest rates as low as on primary residences. Investment loans can be obtained for as little as 10% down (though 20% or more is most common), and the interest rates are somewhat higher.

The general rule is that the more risk you ask a mortgage company to assume, the tougher the rules are going to be for the mortgage you want. Government guaranteed loans (e.g., FHA, VA) take some of the burden off the lender, so that they can keep the rules easier for you to meet. But conventional loans (anything not guaranteed by an agency of the federal government) tend to follow this formula: The more money you put down, and the better qualified you are to repay the loan, the more the mortgage company will be willing to give you good terms and rates.

Interest rates are around the lowest they have been in over 20 years. The political and economic climate in this country has conspired to produce 30-year fixed rates that have hovered in the 5.5% to 7.5% range since 1998. It's at the point where nearly anyone with decent credit and a job can buy a home. You can't always get exactly what you want the first time, but owning, saving, and taking advantage of a growing market may give you the ability to take your increased equity every couple of years and trade into a better home. Many buyers have done just that. The process of buying then trading up every few years is known as stepping-stone buying.

Creative Financing

If you are finding it difficult to get financing through the normal programs, you may have to get creative. Some ideas our borrowers like are the *NIV loan* or *no-doc loan*. With enough money down, usually 20% but sometimes only 10%, you can get one of these loans. NIV stands for "no income verification." It is a loan where the lender feels there is a large enough down payment, and hence they would feel relatively secure if you were to default, so they do not concern themselves with verifying the income you state on your loan application. They may simply verify you are employed where you say you are and you actually have the resources necessary to cover the down payment and closing costs. A *no-doc loan* is a loan where the lender does not require documentation of either income or assets (assets in this case means the money to cover down payment and closing costs). Both of these loans will have a higher interest rate, as much as 1.0% to 2.0% higher than conforming loans. But, when you can't do normal financing, these are still good loans to go after.

Many mortgage brokers also have connections for what are called "B" and "C," or sub-prime, loans. Again, these are loans with higher, sometimes much higher, interest rates. They are designed for people who cannot qualify for normal financing because they are usually high credit risks.

You may also try to find a seller who is willing to finance part or all of the purchase for you. We've often engineered purchases where the buyer only had 10% to put down but needed a 20% down no-doc loan. We would get the seller to carry a second note for the buyer in the amount of 10% of the purchase. Then, with the buyer's additional 10% down, only an 80% primary mortgage was needed. The buyer ended up with two notes to pay off, but the combined payments were usually within a few dollars of what a 90% loan would have been anyway.

Many Realtors® have also identified certain people who have money to invest, and who would like to earn somewhat more than the prevailing 30-year Treasury rate. For 1% or 2% above the current 30-year rate, they are often willing to finance a smaller mortgage themselves. Sometimes, such a loan has a balloon payment, meaning it has smaller payments for a period of time (like five years), and then at the end of that period the entire amount becomes due. For people who have had credit problems in the past, but can demonstrate they are making efforts to clean up their credit, a loan such as this will often get them to the point where they can refinance conventionally, long before a balloon payment becomes due. When a buyer has very little cash to put down, a private lender may take other collateral instead, such as a car or business equipment.

There are many types of creative financing. All of them carry more risk than normal conventional financing, and most will cost more in terms of interest rates. Most, however, do not have financing costs involved (such as loan origination fees, points, and so forth.). Sometimes it's the only way to make a deal work, and if so, you should consider the options. Just make sure you ask a lot of questions and have your Realtor® at your side.

Finally, although it is not likely that an agreement exists making your loan officer your "loan agent," you want to work with one who will, in fact, keep your best interests in mind throughout the financing process. The best place to start is with the Realtor® you have retained. They should be assisting you in this area as well, from lender recommendations to brainstorming sessions to troubleshooting when there are problems. It all centers on that Realtor® and their ability to help get you the best deal.

9. Finding the Right Home

I was just getting my business, Sweet Peas, off the ground and didn't have the time to look for a new home—never mind that it was a necessary activity. You accommodated my schedule so well. Then, after making offers on three—count them, three—homes, I actually got the best of the three for a very good price. As an attorney, I will tell anyone that being represented by a buyer agent is the only way to go. As a business owner, I appreciate the fact that you made sure that all the time we spent together was productive.

—Melanie Kelley

Once you have your relationship established with your Realtor®, and you have your lender on board, you can look for a home with a much better perspective on what you can afford. Whether you are a first-time homebuyer, looking for a second home, or building your real estate investment portfolio, knowledge brings understanding and control to the process. You will also be in a better position when making an offer because you are already preapproved for your loan.

The Search

Your Realtor® will first select homes for you to see from the Multiple Listing Service (MLS). However, a buyer agent is not limited to the MLS. They will probably be aware of new home construction projects and might peruse the classified ads in the newspaper or otherwise be aware of homes being sold directly by owners. Or occasionally, they might have knowledge of a home or two where the owners have not absolutely decided to sell but are considering it. In addition, you might see open house signs or other signs on homes that appeal to you. A word of caution: You have selected a Realtor® and the two of you have an agreement to work together. So, when you see a sign on a house for sale, *do not* call on the sign. Call your Realtor® instead and ask them to do the research, let you know the details, and set a showing if appropriate. Also, ask them how you should handle yourself in open houses. Keep in mind that the listing agent sitting at the open house, or responding to your telephone inquiry from their sign, is usually representing the seller, and they would like nothing more than to keep a buyer's agent from getting a commission by claiming you as "their" buyer.

The homes selected by your Realtor® should generally encompass your stated parameters, including price range, number of bedrooms and baths, general size, garage, and other physical attributes of a home. They will be in your preferred neighborhoods or communities and/or school districts and have other characteristics you have indicated are important. As you look, you may find you cannot put all the things you want together in one package. You can get the home you want, but not in the right school district or neighborhood and so on. You may have to refine your search several times. If you stick to the price parameters established between you, your lender and your Realtor®, then you will probably have to give up some of your preferences. If you are unwilling to give anything up, then you will have to take another look at financing—bringing in a family member to co-sign, working with a partner, or looking for properties in which the seller will carry all or part of the financing.

As discussed in the preface, the perfect home likely does not exist, particularly if this is your first home. Think of it as one step toward that dream home, and listen to your Realtor's® advice about which homes will have better resale value in the future. As we mentioned, many clients have traded up to better homes, often several times.

Recently, a past client approached Ken. When this couple bought a home, they swore they would live in the home for ten or more years. This was exactly where they wanted to be. It was less than two years later, and they wanted him to list their home for sale. But they had second thoughts because they said it would cost them an extra thousand dollars to sell their home. They reminded Ken that when they bought, he said, "I'll bet you a thousand dollars you will not be in this home five years from now. In fact, you will probably move on in less than three years." Ken forgot that bet, and of course they hadn't taken him up on the bet anyway, but it illustrates how people's needs and desires change over time.

There is no way to learn everything about a home before you buy it. You can learn a lot, and we will discuss some of those things here. But the neighborhood, your close neighbors, future plans by the community, are all factors you will discover over time. Your local government may decide to build a highway a few blocks away. Private enterprise may decide to put in a shopping center. Your job situation may change, or you may simply decide you would prefer living in another area for any of a variety of reasons. Very little in this life is permanent. So while you may be perfectly happy with the home you choose to buy, do not be afraid to buy if everything is not perfect.

The key is to start. When you make the change from being a renter to being a homeowner, you will change your life. It is amazing the change in attitude people experience when they actually own the ground they live on. It is the same with businesses. Ken helped Denny, a restaurant owner, who leased the building and land for his business, to purchase the real estate. His restaurant always required more of him than he liked. But recently, when Ken stopped in for a meal, Denny came over to say he'd spent the better part of the day repairing plumbing problems, and he was happy about it. "You know," he said, "before I owned this, I would have raised heck with the landlord and I would have had to pay for the repair anyway, and it would have caused me grief for some time. Now, though it wasn't pleasant working with plumbing pipes, I knew it was my property, and I wanted to see what I could do. Now, it's fixed and I'm happy."

10. Negotiating the Deal

We just wanted to express our gratitude for all of the work you did in helping us with our many real estate transactions since arriving here. With the purchase of three properties and the sale of two in four years (Does that set some kind of a record?), each presented its own challenges. You helped us to obtain our first loan with a quick solution to what seemed an impossible obstacle. You went "all out" to sell our second property with at least five different marketing approaches. And ultimately orchestrated a smooth closing (with about three minutes to spare) on our current home that was almost rescheduled due to new construction delays. Thank you again. We couldn't have done it without you.

—Janelle and Eric Stremel

So you've decided on the right house and you are ready to make an offer. One piece of advice here is to avoid becoming too attached to the property yet. It's nice you have found a home you feel you will be happy in, but you need to be willing to walk away if you can't make the right deal for it. With all the buyers we have worked with through the years, the only ones for whom we could not get any seller concessions were those few who fell in love with the home and the seller would not budge. They were willing to take the home at almost any price. In fact, this piece of real estate had already changed in their minds from simply being a house to being their home.

Assessing Your Position

If you haven't already done it, you and your Realtor® should now prepare for negotiation by formulating a game plan. You should both be clear about what things are vital to have included in the deal and what things you can give up. Most offers should include some unnecessary things you can give up without feeling deprived, while giving the sellers the sense they got a concession from you. It is also important to understand there are many more things to negotiate for than the price. In fact, there are times when price is the least important negotiating objective, and yet price is the one thing nearly every buyer addresses. That is the very essence behind the sticks I discussed in the preface to this book.

For example, if you do not have stellar credit and are unable to obtain conventional financing, you might want the seller to finance for you. In that case, do you really think the sellers, if they will provide financing, will also drop their price? Not normally. Or you may need a really quick close—you will be homeless in two weeks and have to be in your new home. If the new home is empty, you do not have a problem. But if it means convincing the sellers to move out quickly, you may have to concede to the asking price in order to get what you need. On the other hand, you might want new carpet in the deal (and you should ask for it) but could live with the carpet that is in the home now. It is important to know, and to clearly communicate to your agent, those things that are important to you and those that are not.

Always try to negotiate from a position of strength. You can contribute to a stronger negotiating position by getting preapproved for your home mortgage. It will also help if you are making an offer on a home that is clearly within your affordable limits. If you have a home which must be sold first, it will help greatly if you already have a contract by another buyer to purchase that home.

Your Realtor® will also try to find out what might motivate the sellers. While it is not always possible to determine their motivations up front, it is usually worth trying. For example, if you can find out that the sellers are having a new home built, and would prefer not to move out of their present home until the new one is ready, you can address that in an offer. If you are not in a hurry to move, and you can make a closing date or possession date agreeable to the sellers, don't you think they might be willing to negotiate on price?

If appliances are not included in the listing, it is usually because the sellers want to keep them. Your offer should include transferring them to you, even if you do not want them. You could then easily give them up, and may get another concession important to you in exchange.

If you find out that the sellers are being transferred and need to move quickly, or are getting divorced, or are facing foreclosure, you will have accumulated information that is important to your negotiating process.

Once you know as much as you can about the sellers' position, and you and your Realtor® have a clear picture of your negotiating position, you have one last step before preparing the offer.

Determining the Home Value

Before preparing an offer, you should know whether the asking price for the home is above, at, or below market value. This is done by your Realtor® preparing either a formal, or informal market analysis. By identifying other similar properties that have sold recently, determining the sales prices, and determining how those properties differ from the one you are considering, the two of you can readily see if you are starting from a position where you (1) accept the listing price as market value; (2) have to convince the sellers their home is overpriced; (3) need to move quickly with a close-to-full-price offer to get a home priced below market.

In our experience, most homes are priced at or close to market value when a Realtor® is involved. Homes being sold directly by owners are typically overpriced. Usually such sellers not only want to save the sales commissions, but are also either unaware of what true market value is or are trying to push the market themselves. Nine out of ten properties that start out for-sale-by-owner end up listed by a Realtor®.

A home may be overpriced for many reasons. Often, it is just a "trial balloon," where the sellers just want to see if they can attract a better-than-normal offer. There are also real estate agents who "buy" listings. That is, against their own better judgment, they will agree to list a house over market in order to get the listing. These agents may be desperate for business and afraid that they will lose the listing to their competition, or they have been unable to present a convincing argument to the sellers to price their home appropriately.

There are sellers who simply insist their home is worth more than any objective market analysis will indicate. For example, a home which was for-sale-by-owner for months, was overpriced, and now is listed with a Realtor®, may be priced even higher than it was prior to Realtor® representation. That is because the sellers insisted they wanted their net price, so they added sales commissions to the price when they listed the home. This ends up being a collusion between two people, the homeowner and the Realtor®, both of whom are either desperate or greedy and unwilling to face reality. Homes like this usually stay on the market the longest and end up being sold for less than market value.

In the case of an overpriced home, it may be necessary for your Realtor® to include a market analysis with the offer when it is presented.

Homes may also be underpriced for the market. This generally occurs because sellers need to sell fast, or because their agent doesn't have a firm grasp on market value. Sometimes, an agent may convince a seller that the market value is actually lower because the agent wants a quick sale. When you find a property like this, and you determine it is the property you want, do not take a hard negotiating position. Take your Realtor's® advice, recognize the property will be sold fast and offer accordingly. In the past year, Ken sold four properties where the buyer was the first and the only buyer to have seen the property. These were cases where, over time, the buyers could not find the right property, the new listing was underpriced, and it fit the buyers perfectly. Even with fullpriced offers, they got bargains. We check every day for new listings, and when one comes up that fits, we call the buyer immediately to see the property. Remember—*our* buyers get the homes, not someone else.

Negotiating on Price

In general terms, there are two primary approaches to negotiating a deal where price alone is the major consideration. One is to start low and know you will probably reach an agreed-on price somewhere between your initial offer and the asking price. In fact, one of the jobs of your Realtor® is to try to determine the bottom line for the seller. The second approach is to make a "take it or leave it" offer. We generally try this when we have found a home priced above the buyer's ability to pay. If we feel any offer our buyer can make would be lower than what we could negotiate normally, we take the attitude of there being nothing to lose by making the offer. So together we establish the maximum offering price, make the offer there, and inform the listing agent it is a "take it or leave it" offer. Our buyers will not entertain a counter proposal except for "cosmetic" items like the closing date or what is included in the sale. Believe it or not, we had a number of deals accepted on that basis. When the buyer was well qualified at the offering price, offered a quick sale, and the seller was motivated for other reasons, it has worked—and our buyers got properties priced under market.

In most cases, however, you and your Realtor® will discuss a starting point at which to make an offer expecting it to be countered. The idea is to find that point where the seller will sell and you will buy, where each feels they are getting a fair deal, and no one is being taken advantage of.

The vast majority of real estate deals, when both sides are represented, should come down to what is fair. It should end up being a win/win situation, where everyone feels satisfied with the deal. We have all dealt with buyers who "want a deal" and who are unwilling to pay fair market value for any property. They want to steal it, to stick a knife in the seller's back and then twist it. They are only looking for someone who is vulnerable and has to sell at any price. We usually send away buyers like this.

Now, it is true some deals are made like this. We have found properties on the verge of foreclosure, or where sellers have to make a quick sale to save themselves from bankruptcy. We have not hesitated to get one of our buyers into such a deal. But taking the attitude that you can only be happy if you have "screwed" the seller is, in our opinion, corruptive of the whole process of real estate sales.

Usually when the economy is growing and healthy, interest rates are low, but low rates can also occur when the economy is weak and needs to be stimulated. When the market is very competitive, buyers are starting out, moving up, and investing. All of these factors contribute to appreciating values. Sellers and buyers know this and know that a home will, generally speaking, be sold for more today than it would have sold for a year ago. Remember, there are sellers who are trying to "push" the market to get more than their home is worth, and there are agents who will "buy" a listing by telling the seller they can get any price they want. So again, it is important to have chosen a good agent, one who will automatically show you property listings comparable to the one you are interested in which sold recently, and who can tell you if a particular property is overpriced or, as occasionally happens, underpriced.

Remember when something is underpriced, and the home fits your needs, you need to act quickly. Make sure your Realtor® checks new listings every day, and you may be the next buyer who is the only one to see the property. It only takes quick, smart action, and you could own that bargain.

It is also common in a hot market for buyers to lose one, two, or more properties before they get realistic about their offers. It is not smart to make a low offer when your Realtor® has determined the showing activity has been brisk, or competing offers are either in or coming in. Beware, some listing agents will often use the ploy of a competing offer to get you to raise yours, so you cannot always believe it. Then again, a property can sit on the market for an extended period of time with no offers and have two or more submitted about the same time. Even on properties we have listed, we have seen it happen often enough to know it is not necessarily a conspiracy. It is important to have a feel for the market, to know the relative market value of the home you want to purchase and to make an offer that is reasonable to the market.

The Offering Process

Once you and your Realtor® have done your research, they will prepare the actual offer, called a purchase contract or a contract to buy and sell property. Ask your agent for a copy to read ahead of time. When it's filled in you will sign it, write a check for the earnest money, and it will be submitted to the seller or listing broker.

Earnest money is the money that accompanies the offer and signifies that you are entering the contract in good faith. You are putting that money at risk, although not at significant risk. It represents that you are serious about buying the home, you will perform as promised under the offer, and you will come to closing with the balance of the money needed to close the purchase on the home. Some Realtors® place a great deal of importance on the amount of earnest money presented with the offer and feel the more earnest money presented, the better the buyer is.

In the best of worlds, if you have enough money and qualification is not a problem, submitting more earnest money will enhance your negotiating position. If you are a first-time homebuyer, and you are getting a low-down-payment or nothing-down loan, or you are borrowing the money from your parents you may not have much, or any, earnest money to submit with the offer. We have submitted offers for first-time homebuyers with a promissory note as the earnest money. This is when the buyer promises to bring the money to closing, usually out of loan proceeds. We have also submitted offers with minimal earnest money; usually 1% of the purchase price is about the least acceptable deposit. It is then incumbent on your Realtor® to attempt to convince the listing agent and the seller that the minimal earnest money is not a deterrent to your ability to purchase the home.

Your agent, in line with the research you have conducted together, will include one or more "extra" clauses in the contract, which will establish agreements between you and the seller and/or ask for things you would like to have. For example, you might want to have the carpet professionally steam cleaned prior to closing, and a paragraph in the contract could ask for that. If purchasing land on which to build a home, you would probably want to know if a survey, soil tests or other information is available, and you should request that information by a certain date so you can review it. Again, a clause would be inserted to cover that need. There are so many clauses, and so many needs, to cover them all would be impossible. You might review the sampling in the Appendix to see if any of them would work for you.

Once your offer is submitted to the sellers there are three possible responses: (1) The seller accepts the offer as submitted, signs it, and you are under contract; (2) the seller counters your offer with another (called a counter proposal); (3) the seller refuses to respond.

When the seller accepts your offer without question, do not try to second-guess the process. It is not time to worry if you offered too much or gave up too much. If you've done your homework, and you got what you wanted in the deal, be happy. The seller probably has an agent smart enough to advise them that the offer meets the seller's needs and it was not worthwhile trying to squeeze more out of it.

It is absolutely silly, however, for a seller to refuse to respond to a legitimate offer. We will not let one of our sellers ignore an offer. Recently, one of Ken's sellers had a property on the market at $179,000 and an offer came in at $163,000. She reacted to the offer as though it was insulting and would not even respond. This was from a woman who regularly made very low offers on properties when she was the buyer. Ken told her that ignoring the offer was not an option, she hired him to sell her property and part of his responsibility was to ensure he communicates with every potential buyer until they have either bought the property or went away. She said, "Fine, then tell them I'm holding out for full price." He did. Within an hour, the same buyer submitted a new offer at $176,000, and the seller accepted. There are, however, agents who forget their objectivity, become emotionally involved and take offers personally. When reviewing our buyer's low offer, we've had listing agents tell us, with all the resentment they can muster, "This is an insult. My seller won't even respond to this." We find ourselves having to remind the agent they are not the seller, we have a viable buyer who wants the property and is capable of buying it, and if they insist on presenting the offer with the attitude they are displaying, they will run the risk of losing a sale for their seller.

Finally, most offers will elicit a counter proposal from the sellers. The negotiating process continues until you and the sellers have come to agreement on the price, terms, inclusions and exclusions, which work for both of you. If the agents and their clients have done their work responsibly, it should be a deal that makes everyone satisfied, even happy. It will be a win/win deal for everyone.

When everyone has signed on the final counter proposal or redraft of the offer, you and the seller are "under contract." Your earnest money is deposited in an escrow account owned by the real estate broker or by a title company and held until all of the terms of your offer are met and the closing is held. While this process varies from state to state, in Colorado the closing occurs as of a certain date with buyers, sellers, their agents, a lender and a title person all signing the appropriate closing documents. Prior to that time, however, there is work to be done.

11. Inspections, Title Documents, and Other Contingencies

It is much easier, smarter and cheaper to get out of a deal before you close. After the closing, it is most likely to late. Take your due diligence responsibilities seriously, it is some of the best advice I can give.

—Rick Lorenz

The offer you made to purchase property, once signed and agreed to by both you and the seller(s), becomes a contract. A contract is simply an agreement between two or more people (called parties) to do certain things, and in exchange, some form of compensation is paid. In this case, when you do what you have agreed to do in the contract, you get the house. When the sellers do the things they agreed to, they get the money.

Some of the responsibilities of the sellers are:

- providing you with a property disclosure, which is the seller's best representation of the condition of the property and all the fixtures that will be sold to the buyer;
- letting you know if there are any material defects with the property (required by most state laws);
- providing you with a title commitment or an abstract of title;
- providing you with declarations and bylaws, covenants and restrictions, or any other documents which pertain to any home-owner's association or

neighborhood group which might have some say as to what you can and cannot do with your home;

- letting you and certain other people have access to the home for purposes of conducting a home inspection, an appraisal, taking measurements, and so forth;
- answering your legitimate questions about the house; and
- showing up at the appointed time to sign the documents to transfer title of the property to you.

Some of the responsibilities of the buyers are:

- applying for a mortgage loan (if needed) and providing all the information required by your lender to process that loan;
- getting the money necessary to close the purchase—down payment and closing costs;
- providing, and usually paying for, an appraisal to determine the current market value of the property;
- conducting an inspection of the property, usually with the help of a professional home inspector;
- reviewing the title and other documents provided by the sellers and determining if they are acceptable; and
- showing up at the appointed time to take title to the property and pay the sellers.

Nearly every contract has contingencies, which give one party or the other the right to cancel the contract if certain things about the property are not satisfactory to that party or certain obligations of the other party are not met. For example, the loan contingency clause requires the buyer to apply for a mortgage by a certain date and to get loan approval by another certain date. If the buyer's lender anticipates problems getting loan approval, it will be up to the buyers to cancel the contract by the loan approval deadline. In that event, the property will be back on the market. The buyer has the right to review the title and association documents, and by a certain date, if the buyer finds those documents unacceptable, they can cancel the contract and go buy another property. Let's look at some of the major contingencies included in nearly every home purchase contract.

Insurance

Recently, a Realtor® friend reported receiving a termination notice from her insurance company. She had been insured with the same company for over 25 years and had never filed a claim. However, the insurance company "just found out" that she lived more than 10 miles from a fire station.

Another Realtor® friend received a notice from one of his sellers who had recently listed a home for sale. The notice included a copy of a letter received from his insurance company. His insurance was being canceled *because his home was on the market for sale.* The insurance company stated that having one's home for sale presented greater risk due to the fact that strangers will be going through the home.

Almost any property you purchase that requires financing will also require hazard insurance, otherwise known as homeowner's insurance. Your lender will not provide financing without it. However, if you are purchasing a condominium, townhouse or other property that is called a common interest community, this section may not apply. If the property has a homeowner's association that provides insurance on all the units, you will not have to purchase your own coverage to satisfy the lender. However, you will still want to obtain "condo coverage" to insure your contents and, even more importantly, it will give you the liablity coverage you need off of the premises. An example of off-premise coverage would be if you were playing golf and you accidentally hit someone with a ball. Your association would not cover that accident but the condo insurance you obtained would.

Insurance covers you for a number of things, the most disastrous of which is total loss of your home by fire or other calamity. Homeowner's insurance also provides you with liability coverage in the event someone is injured on your property, and it covers you in the event of loss from theft or other smaller mishaps. Interestingly, however, some of the things that most dramatically affect homeowners are being decreased or eliminated from insurance coverage, such as coverage for mold and water leaks. As of this writing [summer 2003], we are facing a national insurance crisis.

The recurring theme of alarm in national, state and local meetings of Realtors® centers on the growing insurance crisis. More and more people are discovering hazard insurance is hard to find or non-existent. There are three primary reasons that insurance companies are refusing to underwrite insurance on new purchases:

1. The seller has either filed a claim, or simply called about a problem, and the insurance company no longer wishes to insure or reinsure the home. The current seller's insurance company could refuse to renew, or the refusal could come from a different company that has been contacted by the seller or buyer. The property may have had water

problems—whether from leaky roofs, broken pipes, runoff or whatever—and the insurance company feels it may happen again or the property may have had mold. The interesting thing is that the homeowner may not have even filed a claim. They may simply have called to see if a situation were covered and if they should file a claim. But, overall, companies feel that properties that have experienced past claims are more likely to experience future claims. The property now becomes, for all practical purposes, uninsurable.

2. The buyer may have had claims on a prior residence that makes the buyer, in the eyes of insurance underwriters, uninsurable. It could be because of similar problems noted above. It could be because a company had to pay a claim because the buyer's previous home was poorly maintained. Companies feel that buyers who have filed past claims are more likely to file future claims. Whatever the reason, the buyer becomes uninsurable.

3. The buyer may have low credit scores. What do low credit scores have to do with homeowner's insurance? Insurance companies have started to underwrite based on their assessment of a buyer's ability to properly maintain their home. In their estimation, people with low credit scores usually are unable to afford routine maintenance, leading the home to fall into disrepair and hence leading to claims-related damage.

Insurance companies are claiming a number of reasons for the current crisis. They point to the $40+ billion in losses in the World Trade Center terrorist attack and to major losses from natural disasters. They point to the surge of mold-related claims that are reported primarily in certain states, but the occurrences of claims are spreading. They call attention to past aggressive low pricing that has resulted in major losses for the companies. What they do not point to, but studies have shown may be the actual reason for their loss of profits, are the losses they have suffered on their investments in the stock market.

The warning is clear. You can no longer take property insurance for granted. As of right now, the past traditional concept of "automatic" insurance is outdated! You must apply for and obtain homeowner's insurance at the earliest possible date in the transaction. Then, if denied by one company, there is at least time to shop for other coverage. You might also work with an insurance broker who works with multiple lines. A broker would have a better idea of where to place the application based on either credit scores or claims history.

What Is a C.L.U.E. Report?

A claims history report on a seller's residence can be obtained from either of two sources. It is called a C.L.U.E. report, which stands for Comprehensive Loss Underwriting Exchange. It is managed and maintained by ChoicePoint and contains information about claims filed on properties in the United States. About 90% of all insurers nationally participate in this exchange.

C.L.U.E. reports are available on properties, not on individuals. So when you make an offer on a property, have your Realtor® insert a clause requiring the seller to obtain a C.L.U.E. report. It will cost them approximately $13, and they can download the report from *www.ChoiceTrust.com,* or request it by mail after downloading the form from that website. If you find the home is determined to be uninsurable, it's much better to know in advance so you have time to work with the seller to check insurability with other companies. There are a few companies that do not participate in C.L.U.E., and a good insurance broker will most likely know them. Mortgage lenders require insurance, so if you are stuck with a property that is uninsurable, you would most likely have to be a cash buyer to purchase the home.

The Colorado Real Estate Commission has developed a new clause to be inserted into buyers' offers. The clause is called *Insurability,* and it gives buyers an automatic "out" if acceptable insurance cannot be obtained. See the sample clauses in the Appendix.

When you first contact an insurance agent, immediately have them check your insurance scores to make sure you are not at risk of not being able to obtain insurance. And once an offer becomes a contract, make sure you apply for and obtain insurance immediately. If you have been denied coverage and received a letter from an insurance company, you can obtain a free copy of your C.L.U.E. report from *www.ConsumerDisclosure.com.* The report will show all claims in the past five years including the nature and the amount of the settlement. Examples could be water or fire damage or dog bites.

This issue of insurance has become so important that the National Association of REALTORS® has appointed an Insurance Task Force to address the growing problem. The task force has already put forth recommendations for state associations to begin working on legislation, to educate their members, and to discover other ways of handling the problem.

The Home Inspection

You normally have the right to conduct an inspection of the home you are purchasing to determine the condition of the home and all the things included in it. This contingency gives you the right to ask the sellers to remedy things that may reduce the value of the home and to terminate the contract if you can't reach agreement with the seller on payment for these repairs.

If you are buying a condominium in a newer project, you may feel comfortable conducting the home inspection yourself. Some of our buyers have plugged a hair dryer into all the electrical outlets to make sure they were working, run the dishwasher, turned on all the burners on the stove, tried the oven, run water in all sinks, baths and toilets to make sure there were no leaks, and checked for other details which could be inspected by observation. Particularly on older properties, many have used professional home inspectors. You and your Realtor® should determine by a review of the condominium documents what things are the responsibility of the homeowner's association. For example, if heat is included in your dues, the association is generally responsible for maintaining heating systems. It is also generally responsible for outside maintenance, including painting, roof replacement, maintenance of common facilities such as a pool or clubhouse and so on. But if the heating system is separate for each condominium, and the individual homeowners are responsible, then you must also inspect the heating system. In that case, you might need a professional.

If you are buying a new construction home (it's being built for you, or you put it under contract before it is completed), the purchase contract is probably full of clauses specially drafted by the seller to protect themselves. Most state-approved sales contract forms do not address new construction, and many of the contracts are unconscionably oriented toward the seller. The best advice for a buyer of new construction is to (1) deal with a builder with a proven track record; (2) review the purchase contract carefully with your buyer agent, and (3) have your lawyer review the contract.

Generally, but not always, you have the right to meet with the contractor shortly before closing on the purchase to inspect the construction. At this time, you will compile what is called a "punch list." This is a list of items that the builder must remedy within a period of time described in your contract. It may include nicks in the wall, broken tiles, doors that do not close properly, and anything else you can identify that needs fixing. The builder will usually have those repairs done after you move in, but within a time period such as thirty days. With new construction, you also have a builder's warranty—usually one year—during which time the builder must fix anything that goes wrong due to faulty construction or materials. You will also have the warranties to appliances and other systems (such as furnaces) included in the house.

There is no automatic right to either a warranty or a preclosing punchlist. Even though they are common, a buyer should carefully check the purchase contract for specifics. Some aggressive sellers, for example, require the buyer to waive all implied warranties in return for a short-term express warranty; this means that if the roof collapses after expiration of the express warranty period, the builder may refuse to repair it. Other aggressive sellers of new construction require the buyer to close on the purchase before the home is ready for occupancy. A certificate of occupancy doesn't necessarily mean that the new home is clean, painted, landscaped, or that the stickers have been removed from the new windows. Again, read the contract with your agent carefully for details on these points.

Unless you are particularly well qualified when you are buying a used home, also called a resale, it is important you hire a professional home inspector to examine the structure. We have even sold homes to general contractors who have hired home inspectors because they realized that even though they know a lot about homes, they do not know all the details of electrical, heating, plumbing or other systems in the homes. Your Realtor® should have a list of qualified home inspectors in the area and be able to recommend some good ones. Because there are no licensing requirements in many states, anyone with little or no training can say they are a home inspector and be completely unqualified. Therefore, limit your inspectors to those who are bonded or insured, or who are members of a certifying organization such as the American Society of Home Inspectors.

A good home inspector has been trained in all the systems and details that make up a house. A good home inspection will take from a couple of hours to a full day, depending on the size and complexity of the house. You should get a complete written report after the inspection is completed. You should always accompany the home inspectors while they are going through the house. Even if the inspector finds nothing wrong with the home, you will learn a lot. Inspectors are great at giving tips on many things. For example, to clean a dishwasher that has a build-up of hard water deposits, empty the dishwasher and use Tang for one or two wash cycles. You will generally learn such things as how to change a furnace filter and how often to do so along with other maintenance functions, which will help you keep your home in good shape during your ownership.

At the completion of the inspection, the inspector may take you through the home just to emphasize what they observed that might need attention. Those are the things you want to discuss with your Realtor®. You may want to ask the sellers to remedy some or all of those items. It's also important to remember that when buying a resale home, it is not going to be perfect. You should not "sweat the small stuff." For example, if all you find in the home inspection is a bath tub or two needs caulking, or furnace filters need changing, or an outside door needs a new weather seal, or other minor details, you might agree to do the repairs yourself or have a maintenance man do them after you move in. However, occasionally the inspector will discover a condition that requires a specialist. For example, they may find a cracked foundation wall which could be due to something more than normal settling. In that case, they might recommend you have a structural engineer inspect the foundation. Other serious items, from the chimney to the furnace, may require different specialists.

It would be appropriate to request that the seller correct the situation if anything major is discovered. If the heat exchanger on the furnace has a leak, it needs to be replaced and that can be a costly item. If any appliance does not work, you may ask it be repaired or replaced. If the roof is in such disrepair, or so old, that replacement is imminent, you may ask the seller to have that work done prior to completing the sale.

When you make your request to the sellers, the sellers may respond in a variety of ways. They may say, yes, they will have the items remedied prior to closing. They may say, no, the price you negotiated on the house does not leave them the money to make the corrections. Or they may offer to settle with you somewhere in between. If they do not have the cash to fix the furnace, for example, but recognize that it needs repair, they may offer to compensate you at closing and let you have it repaired after the home is yours. As long as you and the seller can resolve the inspection items to the satisfaction of both of you, and you put the agreement in writing, you can proceed to closing. If you cannot resolve the issues, you have the opportunity to cancel the contract and move on. In fact, if you find there is a serious, ongoing problem (like the foundation wall), you may want to terminate the contract outright. In Colorado, under many currently approved contracts, you may terminate the contract and give no specific reason other than to say that it did not pass the inspection.

There is one other reason to have a professional home inspection. If you do not, and you discover problems with the home after your purchase, you may have given up your right to make a claim against the seller for those problems. It will depend on the legal issues involved, but almost no one wants to hire an attorney after the fact and spend hundreds or thousands of dollars when the small cost of an inspector would have provided the information you needed in advance. Assuming you have resolved the inspection issues, let's move on to title issues.

Title Documents

The contract will describe certain documents the seller is obligated to provide to you, which are either in the form of a title commitment or an abstract of title. Whichever form it takes, it is a legal picture of the title to the property. It shows you who owns it (hopefully, the seller), the existing mortgage company and the initial amount of their loan. Also, it shows other things about the property that need to be cleared up prior to closing or that might impede your ability to purchase the home.

You and your Realtor® should review these documents to ensure there are no title problems that would prevent you from getting clear title to the property. For example, if there are liens or obligations against the property, which total more than the purchase price, you would want to immediately inquire as to how those debts are going to be paid. Typically, you do not want to take title to a property that has obligations against it which cannot be cleared by the title company at closing. It might be that some of the obligations shown in the title documents have actually been paid, but the payments have not been recorded with the county clerk. A simple recording of those documents would clear those debts from the record.

Some problems might be disclosed in a title search are very simple to remedy. For example, if title is shown to be held in the names of a husband and wife as joint tenants, and one of those persons has died, a simple recording of the death certificate will take that person off the title, thereby enabling the surviving spouse to transfer title to you.

Easements

You will also find things on virtually every set of title documents that will remain with the property even after sale. Utility companies which have power, sewer, water and cable lines running to the property will generally have a continuing easement to go onto your land for purposes of repair, replacement, or installation of their utilities. This is limited to the areas designated on the plat, which is a surveyor's exact drawing of the homesite.

An easement is not an actual title to, or ownership of, property. It is simply a recorded agreement giving access to another person or entity for limited purposes. Local governments might have easements for a variety of reasons, like the access to power poles. Some states may have communities that require setting aside extra land to dump snow off the roadway, or in beach communities it could be for access by the public to reach the water or launch boats. The property you are considering may have an easement giving your neighbor the right to drive across your property to get to their home. Sometimes, it is a shared driveway if they are unable to get reasonable access to their home in any other way. Or, you may have an easement across a neighbor's land.

A buyer should carefully review every easement shown on their title commitment to make sure it will not interfere with their enjoyment of the property.

La Plata County Oil and Gas Issues

When people think of minerals and the Rocky Mountains, their thoughts generally focus on gold and silver mines. While that type of mineral extraction has certainly been historically important, the Rocky Mountains have quickly become the next Alaska or Texas when it comes to natural gas production. Durango, Bayfield and Ignacio are all located in La Plata County, which produces 55 percent of the entire state's natural gas. In particular, the southeast quadrant of La Plata County, which lies in the very north end of the mineral rich San Juan Basin, is reported to contain the largest natural gas discovery in the United States since the 1950s and is currently the second largest active gas field in the United States. This gas field runs from Durango's north end clear down to Albuquerque, New Mexico on the south end of the field. A substantial amount of the current gas production is methane gas extracted from coal beds located several thousand feet below the surface. All across the southern half of La Plata County there are coal beds of methane, substantial reserves of traditional gas types and gas formations in the sandstone. The following information will be very important to you if you are buying in a potential gas reserve area.

First of all, when you buy your property, you are likely not getting the minerals with it. A previous owner, generally the rancher who sold the land off to a developer, kept the minerals years ago. Additionally, in a number of instances the federal government kept some of the minerals when they first offered the land for public purchase back when "the west was settled." Under Colorado law, the surface owner and the mineral owner have certain rights. But case law, especially recently, has indicated the mineral estate to have a superior interest. In almost all instances, the mineral owners have leased their minerals to various gas companies, who then have the right to go on to the surface (which they do not own) to drill wells and install pipelines in order to extract and transport their gas. Furthermore, the lease may grant the gas company the right to construct facilities on the surface. Mineral leases can be signed years before any drilling begins, so the dilemma for you as a buyer generally comes some time later when the gas well is finally installed and the person who received the compensation for the lease is no longer the owner of the surface. The gas company's position is that they are not legally obligated to pay for surface damages. The new surface owner, however, wants to be compensated. In spite of the fact that operators are not obligated to pay for surface damages, many gas operators do negotiate a "surface damage agreement" and are required to consult with you under Colorado Oil and Gas Conservation Commission (COGCC) rules. These agreements may cover surface damage compensation, well-site placement, access road placement and so on.

A separate but equally important issue is whether or not the gas companies can drill a gas well in your backyard. The answer is maybe. Well drilling locations are regulated by the Colorado Oil and Gas Conservation Commission (COGCC) and two issues regarding placement of a well are of particular interest: well spacing and drilling windows, both of which are explained below. For the Fruitland Formation (the coal bed methane gas), the Dakota Formation and the Mesa Verde Formation, the current spacing allows only four wells per square mile. However, it is possible that other types of oil and gas formations could have different spacing rules. Spacing rules tend to change over time, with the tendency being towards allowing more wells so the producer can have a better chance to extract the diminishing amounts of natural resources in the ground. La Plata County has a rule that is especially helpful. In La Plata County, gas wells are not allowed to be drilled within 400 feet of an existing residence. Recent litigation may call that rule into question and it may be better to go with the current COGCC rule of no well within 150 feet of a residence or 350 feet if the area is considered "high density."

Drilling windows are also established by the COGCC. Windows are predetermined areas in which the companies must drill. Window sizes and even their shape vary with the type of formation. Just like spacing can change over time, windows can change as well. Windows range in size from 10 to 23 acres, although there are a very few exceptions that can take the window to nearly 40 acres. A small window (say three acres) would be bad for both gas companies and for the surface owners. What if the undersized window is located on a cliff? Or if the window was in the middle of a river, lake or highway? Let's say you own a 40 acre ranchette and the undersized window was just outside your front porch? Wouldn't you, the landowner, prefer to have them drill on the back of your lot away from the house? Larger windows allow for that type of versatility. To understand how these two features, spacing and windows, dovetail with each other, I'll give you an example. Current spacing (in the year 2003) for the Fruitland Formation is four wells per square mile. That 640 acre square is then divided equally into four 160 acre parcels. Within each of those parcels is a drilling window approximately 23 acres in size. Obviously, the location of the drilling windows can be an important fact to consider before buying a particular home. You can view these predetermined windows on maps to see if the property you like is currently in a window.

Remembering that windows and spacing are not static and that there are a myriad of other rules that may apply to your dream property, we will need some additional assistance in order to make an informed buy or don't buy decision. To help you in this process, I strongly recommend an independent oil and gas land man or an oil/gas attorney. He would review the title documents pertaining to the minerals, the mineral leases, any pipeline agreements and so forth. In addition, he will check all of the drilling windows and spacing orders. Another issue this expert can possibly check whether or not you will get any minerals when you purchase. Title insurance generally does not cover the purchase or acquisition of minerals, so this research expense can be significant. A mineral reservation in a deed needs to be very specific. Over the years, I have found that many drafters of deeds, when preparing the seller's deed, did not properly reserve the minerals to the seller and in doing so, the minerals passed to the buyer. Because the normal mineral lease requires the new owner of the minerals to notify the gas operator of a change in ownership, nothing was ever done. The buyer didn't think he was receiving minerals so he never notified the gas producer and the seller never notified the gas producer because he thought he still owned the minerals. Consequently, he kept getting his royalty check. A mineral expert can discover these types of errors, thus allowing the buyer the possibility of getting a royalty check each month.

A third item to consider is the possible effect gas drilling can have on your domestic water well. My strong recommendation is to have a full spectrographic analysis performed on your well water during the due diligence inspection period. This goes beyond a test for bacteria and would include a test for methane and other possible contaminants. Additionally, a yield test should be performed on the well. It gives you a very good snapshot picture of your water well prior to your purchase. If the water needs treating now, we can negotiate with the seller to take care of it. If it is okay now, but XYZ gas company drills a nearby well two years after closing and your water then changes, at least you have empirical evidence to go to them and say, "My water well has been affected by your gas well operation and I am expecting you to mitigate that problem." I am not saying you will absolutely get compensation, but I can pretty much assure you that without that type of data, you will get nowhere.

A final issue pertains to the amount of surface land a gas well operator can use for free. County rules do not allow drilling on parcels less than 10 acres in size unless the producer receives a waiver to meet certain COGCC rules. With the recent court cases, that county rule is also called into question, but that could change however. For starters, the gas company can build an access road to their well site. Then at the well head, they have the right to exclusively use something over one acre of land (about 204 feet square). When it comes to drilling the well, if the well is going to be drilled fairly near your home, you may want to go visit grandma or the grandkids, as the well drilling process may take two to three weeks. It is an around-the-clock operation and it is pretty noisy and bright. Once the well is completed, assuming it is in the Fruitland Formation, the gas company will likely install a "pump jack." That is that green dinosaur look-alike thing that goes up and down that most people associate with an oil well. In this instance, however, it is pumping the underground water off of the top of the coal until such time as the upward pressure of the gas exceeds the downward pressure of the water, and the gas well then "artesians" just like an artesian water well. At that point the pump jack is removed and the well potentially makes gas for the next 40 or so years. Unless you have a compressor, gas dryer or some other odd piece of equipment on the well site they are pretty quiet and out of mind. There will be some ongoing vehicular traffic to the well site for periodic maintenance and inspection. It would not be your responsibility to maintain their well site nor your job to maintain their road. You may not block or gate off their road without their permission either. Given the demand for natural gas and the political climate both nationally and internationally, it seems that the best solution is to somehow figure out how to coexist as good neighbors. It is the broker's job to make sure you are protected as much as possible and that you are armed with sufficient information to make a fully informed decision.

Neighborhood and Condo Associations

As neighborhoods were established and communities grew, there was not a lot of community planning until the 1960s. When you look at many old cities, you find the types of homes in one neighborhood can be very different from one another. You can find a ranch house next to a modern house or a shack next to a mansion. In the mountains, you often have an "A-frame" next to a large traditional style house. Commercial, residential and industrial components can be randomly interspersed. Over time, governing authorities (town councils and county governments) have usually developed rules and regulations that give them the authority to approve what is built, to ensure some consistency exists in each neighborhood development, and to designate how homes, stores, and industrial development will be separated.

Restrictions on building, both from governments and from developers, have flourished in the past 30 years, but for different reasons. Governments want to control growth and developers want to preserve values.

Therefore, depending on the neighborhood, there may be a set of documents filed with the governing authority by the developer that establish certain guidelines for that neighborhood. These are generally called the covenants, conditions and restrictions (CC&Rs) for that neighborhood. Often these documents will incorporate a set of architectural guidelines, which may be more or less restrictive than local building codes.

If you are buying a condominium or townhouse, the documents are called the declaration and bylaws. Because this type of property is typically managed by a homeowners' association, there will also be a set of rules and regulations. The association collects dues, the amount of which it sets from time to time, and will have a set of financial documents showing how well it has managed the condominium complex.

All of these documents should be provided to you along with the title documents. If they are not, have your Realtor® determine if such documents exist, and if so, have them get copies for you; it is important for you to review them. The restrictions imposed by these documents may be perfectly acceptable to you. For example, some neighborhood associations will not allow anyone to have junk cars parked in front of homes and will not allow you to conduct auto repairs on the property. The restrictions were designed to ensure only certain types of people would live in the neighborhood—those who like the restrictions. If you happen to be a backyard mechanic, this type of neighborhood may not work for you.

Some associations restrict the size and number of household pets. Some condominium associations insist anything stored on your deck (like bicycles) not be visible from the street. All of these restrictions and requirements should be reviewed by the buyer during the title review period. For example, an RV owner would be very unpleasantly surprised if he learned, after closing, that the covenants prohibited RVs from being parked anywhere on the property.

When purchasing a condominium, townhouse, or other property that requires the payment of dues and assessments, you should ask for and review the financial statements of the association. You may also get copies of the minutes of the past two or three meetings. These will help you determine if the association is financially viable—if it has established reserves to cover major periodic maintenance such as roofs, paved parking areas and painting. If reserves are not substantial enough, homeowners could be faced with future special assessments. That is, every homeowner is asked to pay a set amount (sometimes amounting to thousands of dollars) to pay for a needed improvement to the whole complex. If you review the minutes or place a telephone call to a member of the association board of directors, you can also get information about what the association is planning.

These are all things that should be disclosed to you in the title documents. You will have an opportunity to review these documents, and it is important for you to voice any objections before the stated deadline. If there is anything you cannot live with, you will have the right to terminate your contract to purchase the home based on that review. If everything is in order, or at least within your limits of tolerance, then you can move on.

The Appraisal

If you are not paying cash for your property—that is, you are having part of the purchase financed with a mortgage loan—then the loan will generally be contingent on a satisfactory appraisal of value. You have the option of including an appraisal contingency if you are paying cash, but it will be required by the lender if you are financing. Appraisal is a process whereby an experienced professional examines the property you are purchasing, reviews similar properties that have been sold recently, and gives an opinion of the fair market value of your property. However, the appraiser also looks at the contract in place between you and the sellers. If they determine the contract is at a price that is fairly close to the value established by looking at comparable sold properties, they will most likely establish a fair market value at or close to your contract price.

If your contract price is substantially different, then they may establish a fair market value either higher or lower than your contract price. If the appraisal comes in at a value higher than what you have agreed to pay for the home, you can pat yourself on the back, for you and your Realtor® have negotiated a very good deal. If it comes in lower (even by $1), *and* you have made the appraisal a contingency in your contract, you have the right to terminate the contract. The contract can be kept intact, however, by one of three agreements: (1) You agree to pay a larger down payment (because your lender will only lend based on the appraised value); (2) the sellers agree to lower the contract price; (3) you and the sellers agree to settle someplace in between.

If the appraisal does come in low, and you have an appropriate appraisal contingency in your contract, you may have the opportunity to turn away from this deal and go find another home, or to negotiate further with the sellers. Again, you have the chance to decide.

Financing

If you are financing your purchase, there will be a contingency for that. In other words, you are given a certain amount of time for your lender to approve a loan for you within certain established parameters. You may put in the contract that you want a 95% loan with an interest rate no more than 7.5%, with payments over 30 years. In some states, if you do not have full loan approval at terms acceptable to you by the loan approval deadline, you must provide written notice to the sellers to terminate the contract.

If you are having some difficulty getting the loan you want, and a lender suggests another loan that will work, you and your agent may want to negotiate an extension of the contract and establish new loan terms based on the new loan. Whether the sellers agree to cooperate will depend on how interested they are in continuing to work with you. If you do not terminate the contract under the loan contingency, and subsequently you fail to qualify for your loan and cannot purchase the home, you will be considered in default. In many states, if you are in default you will lose the earnest money you paid and additional penalties could be imposed. It is critically important that both you and your Realtor® be cognizant of all contract deadlines and do what is necessary to perform your obligations by those deadlines. Then you will be able to protect your rights under the contract, including your right to terminate, if necessary.

Other Contingencies

Other contingencies can also be built into an offer, the inclusion of which will depend on a variety of circumstances. For example, perhaps you must sell your current home before you will have the money to purchase the new home, and you cannot wait to put the new home under contract. In this case, you will need a contingency stating if you cannot sell your existing home you can terminate the contract on the new home. Usually, if a seller accepts this contingency they will want to put a definite time limit on it.

If you are buying raw land, and have plans to build a home or other building, you will want time to determine what exactly you can build. You may want to meet with planning commissions and other governing authorities to determine if you can build what you want. You may also want to research other aspects of the land. For instance, has toxic waste ever been disposed of on the land? Can you get access? Is it served by an established infrastructure, like water, sewer, gas and electricity, or will you have to establish your own? What others have rights to use the land easements? Can you get the financing you need to build? You may want to use a defined time period to conduct any and all research on the land as you see fit, and if for any reason, you find the land unacceptable, you can terminate the contract. This is called a "due diligence" contingency.

If there are special problems with the property, you may want to engage the sellers' efforts to have those problems removed and make your offer contingent on the successful accomplishment of that action. For instance, if a neighbor has an outbuilding or driveway that encroaches on the property you want, you may ask the sellers to take the steps necessary to eliminate the encroachment. You clearly do not want to inherit a problem, and because the sellers presumably have an established relationship with their neighbors, it might be relatively easy for them to get this accomplished. Often, conditions like this may not be discovered until you receive and review the title documents. While title documents address these issues in general, you may want to amend the contract to specifically address those things you want resolved as a condition of going forward.

There may be other contingencies that make sense to incorporate into your contract or into an amendment to it, and all the relevant circumstances should be discussed with your Realtor®. Be careful not to incorporate frivolous contingencies because they may make the contract unattractive to the seller, but intelligently drafted contingencies could mean the difference between disaster and success.

12. Getting to the Closing Table and Moving In

> I am writing to express my appreciation for the manner in which you assisted me in my search for a home. I also wish to commend you for your efforts in the subsequent negotiations prior to the closing of the purchase. Thanks to you, the entire process went smoothly and was completed without a hitch or a hang-up. The thirty-minute closing, from the time we walked to the table until we walked out the door, must be some kind of record.
>
> —Mark Kelley

By now, you might be feeling as if you've completed a college course, and that's understandable. This book gives you some idea of just a few areas a Realtor® has to learn to navigate in this business. It seems easy because we do it every day. Of course, most transactions are fairly normal, predictable events where the standard actions are taken, nothing out of the ordinary is discovered, no financing problems exist, title documents are clean, the inspection is uneventful and everyone comes to the closing table happy. However, we have to always be prepared for the worst.

We've covered a lot of potential disasters in this book, but there are more. Real estate transactions, when complicated by whatever reason, tend to take on their own personality and character. Every Realtor® has experience with deals that fell apart and didn't close, sometimes at the last minute. When that happens, the people involved are usually pointing fingers, often blaming the nearest or most convenient target.

The Sale That Didn't Happen

One of Ken's earliest transactions involved Julie, a single mother who was selling her home and buying another. The home Julie was selling was called a "cluster home"—that is, it was located in a home project governed by a homeowners' association. It was just like a townhouse or condominium project, except the homes were all detached. For Julie's soon to be "former" home another agent had produced a buyer and it was under contract. In addition, Ken found a home Julie wanted and put it under contract for her. Everything was going smoothly, except the lender for the buyers of Julie's former home did not get loan approval on time. Ken spoke with the lender every day and was assured the loan would be approved, even though this home purchase was at the maximum the buyers could handle. Their credit was fine, and the ratios were close but acceptable, but the underwriter was just overloaded so they waited. Julie and her kids packed and scheduled a moving company.

On the day they were supposed to close on both the sale of Julie's old home and the purchase of her new home, with the house full of packed boxes and the moving van parked outside, Ken got a call from the lender. The loan had been denied for the buyers. It seems the lender did not notice there were homeowners' association dues involved with Julie's home and did not include that information in the loan package. Of course, he blamed Ken for not informing him of that fact. However, this information was detailed in the contract, which is one of the first loan documents provided to the lender. Ken simply referred him back to that contract.

Well, it was a disaster. The number of people negatively affected was enough to cause a relatively new real estate agent to quit the business before any more people were hurt. The buyers' lease had ended, and they had to move out of their apartment, now with no place to go. Julie and her two children had to stay in their old home and live out of boxes until Ken could get it sold again. The sellers of the home Julie was scheduled to buy wanted to keep her earnest money because they were so angry, but Ken had the sale of Julie's home as a contingency in the contract and she got her money back. When Julie's purchase fell through, those sellers had to cancel their pending purchase of another new home. And, although not very important to all of the frustrated home purchasers and sellers involved, none of the real estate agents involved in any of the transactions got paid. They all had to do their work over again.

Ken kept telling Julie through her tears that things happen for a reason in this world, and they would get her house sold and find her an even better home to move into. And that actually happened. When it was all said and done, she had a house far superior to the one she would have bought, in a nicer neighborhood, closer to the schools her children would attend, and she ended up happy. But what a process getting there! We wouldn't wish that to happen to anyone.

That is why we build in contingencies to contracts, and we try to cover all the bases so everything that is promised actually occurs. For example, every contract should have a clause that lets you go into the home one or two days prior to closing to do a final walk-through. This lets you verify that the home is in at least as good a condition as it was when you put it under contract, and the sellers have done those things they promised. For example, if your contract called for having the carpets professionally steam cleaned (note the language—you generally don't want to settle for the sellers renting a do-it-yourself cleaner), you can make sure that was done. If they were to have certain things repaired or replaced as a result of the inspection agreement, you can verify that those items were completed.

Keep in mind, typically, there is nothing in the contract that obligates a seller to actually clean the house for you. Usually, it is common courtesy to do so, but if that is important to you, put it in the contract. You see, contracts simply keep everything nice and tidy. If everyone you dealt with were completely honest, had an impeccable memory, and always had it in their heart to do the right thing, contracts probably wouldn't be necessary. But even honest people have short memories, or get in a hurry, or decide they already gave too much, which is why we have contracts.

Bring your Realtor® with you to do your walk-through. Bring to the listing agent's attention anything that wasn't completed according to the contract and have it corrected prior to closing. Ultimately, you hold the trump card. You have the money to hand over at the closing table, and if everything was not done as agreed, you can say, no, you're not going to close. Now, practically speaking, that rarely happens, and everything is in place to close. You probably have packed or otherwise made plans to move out of your current residence, you are excited about being in a new home, and the pressure is on everyone to go ahead and sign. So again, don't sweat the small stuff.

Anything significant could be handled with a written agreement at closing, or by setting aside additional money in escrow. For example, let's say the seller was to replace the furnace but could not get a repairperson in to complete that job in time. You could all agree to have the title company or escrow company withhold the money for that item from the proceeds that are due to be paid to the seller. The title or escrow company would then pay the repairperson when the work was complete. Or if the carpet was supposed to be cleaned but wasn't, the seller could hand you a check at closing so you would have the money to pay for it.

What do you do if the seller refuses? You have to decide. Is it more important to close, or should you walk away? We're not telling you this because it happens often, but because it does happen occasionally, it's best to be prepared.

If your transaction is typical, everything will have been completed per agreement, you sign the closing papers, present your check, and get the keys to the house. Everybody walks away with big grins on their faces, looking forward to the new life they have created.

Now for the fun part—It's time to move in.

Part Five

Other Considerations

13. Mining Claims

As I mentioned earlier, most people think of gold and silver mines when they think of the Rocky Mountains. A "mining claim" is the vehicle that was invented by the U.S. Congress to deal with the unique situation of locatable minerals. The best way to describe what mining claims are is to give you an illustration that is pretty much universally understood. Years ago, the U.S. government wanted the West settled by pioneers. As a result, Congress created the "Homestead Act." If a family moved west and settled on a 160 acre parcel of land and did certain things to it (cleared it, farmed it, built their home on it and so forth) for a certain number of years, then the U.S. Government would give them a "Homestead Patent" or deed for their efforts. There was a small fee paid to the government as well. However, after that point in time, the homesteader's obligation to farm it, maintain it and so on ceased. The land was the owners to do with as they chose. *Patent* simply is another word for a "deed" from the U. S. government. Essentially, the ownership of most rural lands west of the Mississippi River originated from homestead patents.

Mining claims, like homesteads, were created by a worker, (in this case a prospector looking for gold, silver, lead, zinc, copper and so on), who would go into the mountains and "stake his claim." At this point the mining claim is called an "unpatented mining claim." The owner of an unpatented claim has the exclusive rights to the minerals within the claim but does not have exclusive rights to the entire surface. After staking the claim, the miner is required to perform a certain amount of work to the property each year, called *assessment work* (tunnels, roads, panning for gold and so on), in order to "prove" his claim was valuable and mineable. The standard was as follows: "Could a reasonably prudent man make a living from this property?" Remember that this was being done during an era of "let's go settle the West" ideology, so "reasonably prudent" was very often liberally construed. Today, it is nearly impossible for a private individual to take a mining claim through the complete process of turning an unpatented claim into a patented one. So long as the prospector meets the standards passed by Congress, he is awarded a "mining claim patent" for his land. At this point he, like the homesteader, no longer has to perform his due diligence to the property. The land could be bought, sold and traded and the owner could build a house, hotel or, as is the case in many Colorado mountain towns, a ski area or two. Unless you are a serious miner and are getting very specialized counsel, do not buy unpatented mining claims as you do not get full title to the property as you do with a patented claim. Buy only patented ones.

What Do You Get when You Buy a Mining Claim?

Unless previously reserved by a prior owner or the government, which would be very unusual, you get full title (fee simple absolute) to the surface and the minerals. Title to mining claims can be passed by general warranty deed and title insurance is available as well. However, remember that most title insurance companies do not insure the title to the minerals. In the Durango and Silverton area, I am able to get mineral coverage for an increased fee, generally paid for by the seller as part of the negotiations. Just like any other land, mining claims are subject to the county building and zoning regulations. One particular issue of major importance is legal, insurable access. Many mining claims, due to their mountainside location, do not have roads to or through them. Consequently, that is an issue that needs to be carefully examined during the due diligence process.

There Are 3 Types of Mining Claims: Lode, Placer and Millsites

Lode claims tend to be 300 feet wide by 1500 feet long, which would net 10.331 acres. Ideally, the miner's "vein of gold" runs the full 1500 feet in length and he can follow it underground to the center of the earth. He cannot mine beyond either of the end lines (the 300 foot ones). These are properties where the owner is tunneling into the rock, drilling and blasting to move the rock. Excavations that are horizontal are called tunnels or drifts. Excavations that go down into the ground are called shafts. Excavations that mine upward or vertically are called stopes.

Placer claims do not have a definite shape and can be much larger (I have seen up to 120 acres). These are "staked out" around rivers and streams, and are the kinds of claims where a miner "pans for gold" as often seen in western movies.

The last type of claim is a millsite. When miners blast all of the rock and end up with ore, they need to process that ore to efficiently extract the gold, silver, lead, zinc, copper and so on. That work is done on a millsite. These sites are not over five acres in size. With all three claims, once these properties are patented, the owner no longer needs to do his "assessment work" (the term applied to all of the preliminary work required to obtain the patent) and can use them as he so desires. Mining claims often "overlap" another mining claim. Although that seems unusual, overlapping is almost always the norm with mining property. Remember that the miner staked the claim so the vein would run the 1500 foot direction on his property. Suppose another vein a hundred or so feet away takes a turn and crosses over the first vein? This happens all the time. The answer to who owns the "overlapping" area lies in the actual patent signed by the President of the United States.

By their very nature, mining claims are located in the rugged mountains because that is where God put the minerals. Consequently, claims tend to be steep with maybe a building spot or two for a nice cabin or camping site. Views tend to be spectacular, particularly if you come from the flatlands back east. Many claims are located above timberline (roughly 11,400 feet) and electricity is pretty rare. As to their exact locations on the ground, all of the claims have to be surveyed by a U. S. Mineral Surveyor in order to obtain the patent. Often times those original corners (usually a 4x4 post set in the middle of a pile of stones) are gone, so a new survey would be required if you wanted to know the exact boundaries.

14. Real Estate and the Internet

Mollie Wasserman's Real Estate Internet Warning©

Despite advertising claims to the contrary, the Internet is *not* an experienced real estate professional. It cannot consult, counsel, advise, have knowledge of local laws and market conditions, make judgments, "own" the result, or most importantly, understand your individual goals and needs and care about you as a client. Furthermore, data by itself can be very misleading. To obtain an accurate interpretation of any information you're receiving online, please contact a Realtor®.

— Mollie Wasserman

Given the revolution in technology that we've experienced over the last few years, we must look at *what technology can and cannot do*. This differentiation is especially crucial when dealing with real estate, an environment where online companies clutter the bandwidth and your inbox with schemes to save incredible amounts of money and time by using their services.

Now let's be clear: Technology, and specifically the Internet, is a wonderful thing! Technology is a fabulous way to gather data and can do *functionary* tasks better, faster, and cheaper than any human being ever could. But the danger does not lie in understanding that technology. The danger is that, by itself, the Internet can never provide the *fiduciary* counsel required in services such as mortgage lending, law, and real estate.

Functionary/fiduciary—why do we keep using these "f" words? Simply, it's very important to understand the difference between the data that you can get online and the advice, counsel, and interpretation of that data, that only your Realtor® can provide if you're to get the best deal when you buy or sell a home.

Information Versus Knowledge

As Internet-savvy Realtors® who generate a significant portion of our business online, we are big believers in the free flow of information. You will find that both online and off, this new breed of Realtor® usually provides the most complete sources of information that you'll find anywhere.

Yet, we have had many of our colleagues question why we give out so much information, often saying: "If you give out too much information, people will have no reason to call you." We disagree. Although we give out information freely, we have never had a shortage of requests to retain our services. That's because there's a big difference between *information* and *knowledge*.

John Tuccillo states in his book, *The Eight New Rules of Real Estate,* "Information is a collection of facts or observations about reality. Knowledge is actionable." In today's information age, consumers can increasingly get all the information that they want or need, but it's useless unless someone with expertise in the field can provide the knowledge to allow them to correctly act on it. *Information, without the context of a pro who can share the day-to-day knowledge of the industry, is just* data. *If a consumer were to act on it without context, they could very well reach incorrect conclusions and achieve undesirable results.*

Information is like sand on a beach—it's plentiful and anyone can find it. But if you want to build a sandcastle, you may want to consult the Sandmaster who lives on the beach. They could tell you how much water to use, what weather conditions are best for building, and most importantly, when the tide comes in and how far up. Without this knowledge, you could spend an entire afternoon building a great sandcastle, only to have it washed away!

Myths Involving Real Estate and the Internet

People definitely love to surf the Internet when it comes to real estate. It's estimated that last year, between 70 and 80% of homebuyers started their search online. But there are definitely myths about what the Internet can and cannot do. The following myth is one of our favorites:

"The Internet is great! I can . . .

1. buy a book
2. buy an airline ticket
3. buy or sell a house
4. get legal advice
5. receive a medical opinion

. . .*all* online!"

At what point in the above statement did it step over the line from fact to myth? If you say after number two, the airline ticket, give yourself a gold star! What's the difference between the first two products and the last three services? Simple. *The first two are commodities bought mostly by price, the last three are services that require counsel, advice, knowledge, and understanding of your individual needs*. The first two are functionary products, the last three are fiduciary services. You can purchase the first two products entirely online and probably save money in the process. In regard to the last three services, the Internet is a great place to start your search for service providers. But if you try to "go it alone" with just the data you find online, you will very likely risk losing your shirt if you don't consult a local provider who understands your individual needs and is accountable for their services.

Let's look at a couple of obvious examples before turning to real estate. Let's say there's an online site called Weknowlaw.com. For $39.95, payable in advance by credit card, you can receive a "legal opinion." Does this opinion come from an attorney, a paralegal, or a truck driver?

The site says it's from an attorney, but how do you know for sure? And what if you take this legal advice and your case turns out badly? How do you get out of the deeper legal dilemma you're now in? Local attorneys who are dependent on referrals for future business have a great incentive to stand behind their advice and counsel. Does whoever at Weknowlaw out there in Dot-Com Land care if you're unhappy with their opinion?

In other words, what happens if something goes wrong?

Then there are the online mortgage companies that advertise everywhere. If you've read the business section of the paper lately, you know that many of these companies are not doing so well. Why is this? Well there are a couple of reasons. First, much of the mortgage process still has to be done locally, so there's little economy to doing the process online, and more importantly, many consumers are finally catching on that interest rates and financing programs are very vulnerable to the old bait and switch that we mentioned earlier. Do you really think for a moment that the online mortgage company in Anywhereland is particularly concerned if you're unhappy with their services? A local mortgage lender derives business from local Realtors® and the community.

Therefore, they have to make the situation right because they must be *accountable*! The national dot-com isn't. Now, as we said earlier, the Internet is a wonderful place to shop rates and programs and to educate yourself on the mortgage process. But afterwards, do yourself a favor and bring the best package to your Realtor's® recommended lender and ask if they can match it. Either they will, or they'll tell you why they can't.

Have you ever been to a medical website? There are many wonderful sites out there. If you were to go to one to become a more educated patient, and then take your questions and concerns to your doctor, that would be a very smart use of the Internet. If, however, you were to go to a site and attempt to diagnose yourself, that would be a very unintelligent use of information, with potentially disastrous results.

Real estate is an interesting field in that it combines functionary tasks with fiduciary counsel. Functionary tasks such as property searches or accessing home sales data can always be done cheaper, faster, and better by technology. If that was the whole of real estate, we'd be the first to applaud the national dot-coms popping up online promising to provide you these services without your having to leave the computer. But the problem is, these companies don't tell you what you *don't* get. As an example, there are a couple of companies that heavily advertise that you can get a *free* home valuation online. All you have to do is give them a street address and it's yours. So what *do* you get? (Drum roll please.) A list of homes sold within a one-mile radius of that address. Does this "home valuation," coming from a national site, take into account the power plant going in two blocks away from this home, which will affect its value? Has it seen the inside of the home to find out how it compares with others? Does it take into account the railroad tracks on the next street? What about the local economy and the fact that young professionals are moving into the area, accelerating the increase in prices? What about sewer abatements or the newest regulations? A national dot-com can't advise you of any of those things, which could greatly affect the value of the property; but a Realtor® who's working in your interest can.

Of course, many buyers aren't ready for a relationship with a Realtor® right off the bat. When you're just starting the process, you may want to get your feet wet by getting property listings and doing "drivebys" of homes that look interesting before interviewing Realtors®. That's understandable. That's why many Realtors® offer their website's Property Search and Daily Email Alert services to nonclients for a 60-day trial membership. At the end of 60 days, however, nonclients usually must schedule a buyer consultation or lose access to the service. This policy is not intended to be unhelpful, but we know that there's a lot more to successfully buying a home than property listings. Simply providing housing information without interpreting it based on the buyer's goals and timetable is not going to get a buyer their best deal.

Please remember that while the Internet can provide information, it cannot interpret it! A Realtor®'s value is not in finding you a home, though we certainly have the tech tools to help you there. Our real value is in helping you get your best deal on a home once you've found it!

If you have more questions about real estate and the Internet you can also contact Mollie Wasserman at mollie@MollieW.com.

To Reach Rick Lorenz
Address: 901 Main Avenue
Durango, CO 81301
Phone: (800)955-0259 ext. 145
(970)-375-7007
Fax: (970) 259-5007
Rick@BuyDurango.com
www.BuyDurango.com
www.DurangoColoradoHomes.net or
www.DurangoVirtualTour.com

To Reach Ken Deshaies
Mail: P.O. Box 37-330 Dillon Ridge Rd., Suite 6
Dillon, CO 80435
Phone: (888) 221-SNOW
Fax: (866) 782-6059
www.SnowHome.com

To find out if you can become a
published author, visit:
www.GabrielBooks.com
or email rennie@GabrielBooks.com

APPENDIX A

Sample Clauses for the Contract to Buy and Sell Real Estate

Note: Language in these clauses has not been approved by any Real Estate Commission. They are provided as examples only and are meant to bring your attention to issues that you might want to address in your offer to purchase. Your Realtor® may use similar or dissimilar language to accomplish the same result. Consult with your Realtor® or your attorney on the use of any language in your contract. Or contact the authors for a referral to someone in your area.

Sample Clauses

Note that the use of an asterisk (*) in any clause below indicates the need for information. You and your Realtor® should determine the information—number or data—needed in each instance. Of course, you should also discuss the applicability of any of the following, or other, clauses before finalizing an offer.

Buyer's Right to Change Financing

Buyer reserves the right to change loan programs as long as the net proceeds to Seller under this contract remain the same.

Working Order

Seller represents that all of the appliances, systems, and utilities servicing the property will be in working order at the time of delivery of possession to Buyer.

Automatic Extension

In the event Buyer's loan has not been approved by the deadline set in Section * due to delays in loan processing caused by parties other than the Buyer, then loan approval, closing and possession deadlines shall automatically be extended for up to * calendar days.

Carpet Cleaning

Seller will have the carpets professionally steam cleaned within 48 hours prior to closing if the property is occupied, or anytime prior to closing if the property is and will remain unoccupied until closing.

There are times when, for convenience or expedience, you may make an offer individually, fully intending to take title in the name of a company or to add a spouse or other partners. If so, consider the following:

Assignability of Contract

Notwithstanding the provisions of Section * herein, Seller acknowledges that Buyer intends to form a company prior to closing in which name Buyer intends to take title. This will not release Buyer of the obligation to provide financial information to Seller, and Buyer agrees to sign individually on any loan herein.

—or—

Notwithstanding the provisions of Section * herein, Seller acknowledges that Buyer intends to add one or more partners to this contract prior to closing, and that title will be taken in the name(s) of all partners. This will not release Buyer of the obligation to provide financial information to Seller, and Buyer agrees that Buyer and additional partners will each sign on any loan herein.

When you are selling an investment property and replacing it by purchasing another through a 1031 exchange, consider the following:

Section 1031 Exchange

Seller shall cooperate in structuring this transaction as a like-kind exchange for the benefit of Buyer, as long as Seller incurs no additional cost. Despite the anti-assignment provision of Section * herein, Buyer has the right to assign its rights and obligations under this contract to an entity acting as Qualified Intermediary (as defined in Internal Revenue Code Section 1031) to complete the like-kind exchange, but assignment shall not release Buyer from liability for performance of any of its obligations. In the interest of convenience, however, Seller shall convey title to the property and inclusions directly to Buyer on behalf of the Qualified Intermediary. This subsection is not intended to waive any of the deadlines or other obligations of Buyer in this contract. Buyer acknowledges being advised to seek the guidance of tax counsel in completing this Section 1031 Exchange.

When you have to sell one property in order to purchase another, it is incumbent on you to solicit the seller's cooperation, both for the sale and, ideally, for the coordination of closing dates. The following two clauses may help:

Sale of Buyer's Other Property

Buyer shall have the right to terminate this contract at any time prior to * if Buyer has not sold certain "other property" owned by Buyer and described as *, on terms acceptable to Buyer. If Buyer has not given Seller written notice of said termination by the deadline in this subsection, Buyer shall be deemed to have waived this contingency. If Buyer does not sell the other property by the deadline and does not terminate this contract as provided in this subsection, and if this contract then fails to close because Buyer fails to qualify for any financing described in Section 4b, Buyer shall forfeit to Seller all earnest money deposited hereunder. If Buyer does not have the other property under contract and does not provide Seller with a copy of the executed contract by *, Seller shall have the right to terminate this contract by giving written notice to Buyer within five days thereafter. Seller may continue to market the property. If, prior to the deadline in this subsection, Seller receives an acceptable bona fide offer from a third party to purchase the property, Buyer shall have three calendar days following notice thereof in which to either waive this contingency or to terminate this contract. Failure by Buyer to elect one of these two options shall be deemed a waiver of this contingency.

Change and Coordination of Closing

Seller hereby agrees to change the closing date herein and coordinate same with the closing of Buyer's other property, should a contract to purchase the other property designate a closing date other than that set herein. Buyer agrees to make a good faith effort to negotiate a closing date on said purchase contract to match the closing date herein. If Buyer is unable to do so, however, Seller agrees to extend the closing herein by up to * days if necessary to make such closings happen on the same day.

Notes

Order Form

Regarding the REALTOR® titles, we have many different state editions for homebuyers across the country. Even though they may be location-specific due to different state laws, the concepts hold true in any area. All of the buyer agency books are priced at **$17.95 each**. If you are looking to buy a home, please see our current state editions at our web site: **www.BuyerAgency.net**

To sell your home for the best possible price, buy a copy of:

Get the Best Deal When Selling Your Home, Denver, Colorado Edition, by Debbie Moore and Ken Deshaies $18.95

To order any of our books you can write to us directly, contact your local bookstore, FAX, or order online at: **www.GabrielBooks.com**

For additional information, please call (800) 940-2622.

Additional Books for Financial and Business Growth:

Couples and Money, by Victoria Collins, PhD $13.95

A vital guide for couples to thrive financially and emotionally. It provides exercises and instructions for couples to talk about money. Recommended by Consumer Credit Counseling Service.

Wealth On Any Income, by Rennie Gabriel, CLU, CFP (UCLA Instructor) $17.95

Move from creating financial goals to achieving them. Covers both the emotional and practical aspects of handling money effectively. Endorsed by Mark Victor Hansen, co-author of the *Chicken Soup for the Soul*® series.

Wealth On Any Income cassette tape program $59.00

Five hours read by Rennie Gabriel from his book. It is a comprehensive but simple to use program for anyone to handle money effectively, get out of debt, live within their income, start investing with as little as $100 and ultimately create financial independence. Includes full book and two spending registers.

Money Talk, by Todd Rainey $17.95

A gay and lesbian guide to financial success including partnership agreements and health care powers.

How to Outwit and Outsell Your Competition, by Shirley Lee $14.95

Grow your business 50–200% per year using little-known, powerful strategies that cannot fail. Avoid costly marketing blunders by learning the common mistakes.

Order Form—Please Copy, Fill Out, Mail, Fax, Phone or Go Online

Name______________________________________

Address____________________________________

City, State, Zip_______________________________

Daytime Phone (__)____________________________

Email Address_______________________________

Product Description	Quantity	Total
____________________	______	$______
____________________	______	$______
____________________	______	$______
____________________	______	$______
Sales tax, 8% (only for orders delivered in CA)		$______
Shipping and handling, $4 per book or tape		$______
	Total:	$______

❑ check enclosed $______________________________

❑ please charge my M/C or Visa #__________________

Expiration date______________________________

Signature as on the card_________________________

Mail to: Gabriel Publications
14340 Addison Street #101
Sherman Oaks, CA 91423-1832
or fax to (818) 990-8631
www.GabrielBooks.com